Image BEARER

Image Bearer

Venner Alston

Image Bearer by Venner Alston
Published by VJ Alston International Ministries
10936 N Port Washington Road, Suite 226
Mequon, WI 53092
www.drvjalston.org

Visit the author's website at www.drvjalston.org
International Standard Book Number: 978-0-9908585-0-8
E-book ISBN: 978-0-9908585-1-5

20 21 22 23 24 — 987654321
Printed in the United States of America

CONTENTS

Chapter 1

THE POWER OF IMAGERY

But we all, with open face beholding as in a glass the glory of the Lord, are changed into the same image from glory to glory, even as by the Spirit of the Lord.

—2 Corinthians 3:18

If I take a picture of you, is the photo actually you? No, it's an image of you. Image is one of the most powerful mediums in our world that helps us to connect with ideas, feelings, each other, and just about any tangible or intangible sense. *Image* is defined as "a reproduction or imitation of the form of a person or thing"; it is "the optical counterpart of an object produced by a device as a lens or a mirror or an electronic device"; it is "a likeness of an object produced on a photographic material."[1] It is also "a mental picture or impression of something," an "exact likeness," or "tangible or visible representation" of something. This means that an image can be something that is tangible, something that is real and in front of us like a statue. It can be something that is a representation of a real thing, like the photograph of you we just mentioned. It can also be something we can visualize in our minds, something we recall by memory and see, or something we use our imagination to draw up.

Let's try it now and see how it works. Close your eyes. Take time to see the following images in your head:

- See yourself taking a bite of a shiny, red apple—and it is so crisp.
- Now think of a black and white spotted dot.
- Imagine a lion roaring.
- Visualize a yellow banana.
- Can you get a mental picture of a pink shirt? Does it have buttons or is it a pullover?
- What about big slices of juicy, red, ice-cold watermelon on a hot day?
- Can you imagine eating a nice, thick, perfectly grilled steak, with sautéed mushrooms and onions, a little rice on the side, with some hot biscuits and gravy?

Now open your eyes. How did you do? Were you able to see each image in your head? If you were, then your ability to see images in your head is well developed like most of us. You were able to draw up a mental picture of the things I called out but realize that obviously you were not looking at the items themselves. They were not concrete or part of your tangible reality. This is imagery created in your mind by your imagination, which is "the act or power of forming a mental image of something not present to the senses, or never before wholly perceived in reality"; it is "a creation of the mind."[2] What you saw was not actually there, but sometimes images can be so strong that you can taste them in your mouth. You can smell them with your nose. Or feel their texture or presence with your skin.

When I asked you to visualize the meal with "hot biscuits," you already had your honey, jelly, or whatever you put on your biscuits, ready to pour or smear over them. You could probably smell the butter and feel your mouth begin to water. But again, these images are mental images not images that are actually present to your external senses.

The extent to which we can use our imagination is part of the creative ability God gave to us. But for everything that God has given to us, the enemy tries to corrupt it and use against us. Let's hold this thought for a moment.

By Beholding, We Become...

We need to have a clear understanding of how powerful an image is, how much we respond to it, and how it drives the choices that shape our lives. By God's design, we are very visual. According to one expert, "Almost 50 percent of our brain is involved in visual processing and although we have five senses, 70 percent of all sensory reports are in the eyes."[3]

Vision is our primary sense. We can see something, analyze it, and attach meaning and purpose to it in less than one-tenth of a second.[4] In other words, we see something and make split-second decisions about where it belongs in our lives. We attach various levels of importance to the things we see. We determine the image's relevance and value to our lives or to the thing we are doing at the moment. Our brain cells fire up to 2 billion times per second just to compute, integrate, and remember all of the visual information we take in through our eyes.[5]

Advertisers hinge their client's success on how humans process visual images. They spend billions of dollars researching how to move and manipulate our decision centers so that we buy their products or engage with their brands. They know that the more we see the same image, the more likely we are to give it more space in our brain. The more we see an image, the more value we place on it. The more it begs for our attention, the more we yield our attention to it. The more attention we give it, the more likely we are to do what we see it do.

They've studied the fact that even more than what they tell us, what they show us has a greater impact on us identifying with them to the point of becoming consumers and fans.

Think about this: we only remember 10 percent of what we hear, and it takes us twice as long to process and recognize the words we read versus the images we see. But if an image accompanies the sound or words, our recall and recognition increase by 65 percent.[6]

Taking it beyond the image itself, beautiful, striking, and embellished images make a bigger impression on us than just plain images. Imagine the difference between a plain PowerPoint presentation—no graphics, no color, and no visual images to support the content. Seems pretty boring. Now imagine a vibrant, well-organized presentation with large colorful images to break up the information. Maybe some charts and graphs help to get the point across. Which presentation do you think will stick with you? Which one will you remember the most information from?

You probably don't have to do much imagining here. We've all sat through dry presentations and we've attended really good ones. Therefore, we know that the quality of the image, along with the frequency at which it is seen, plays an important part in how well we receive and are impacted by the image.

Reset Your Sights

Image is powerful, and we have underestimated the effect it has on our lives. Many times, we condemn ourselves for being so moved by what we see. We take to the extreme verses about plucking out our eyes if we are given over to lust, adultery, and the like (see Matt. 18:9). Other times, we can become harsh and religious telling ourselves that if we can't believe without seeing we aren't operating by faith.

On one level, we need to be vigilant about what we allow to come into our view and that walking in faith is indeed sometimes walking into the unknown. However, I believe we are in a season where we need to operate with a fuller and clearer revelation on the power of image and the importance of godly images, instead of throwing the whole thing out, shutting down our vision, and guilting ourselves for being so influenced by what we've seen. We need to be thinking, "How can I harness the power of my vision? What does God want me to see?" We also need to be thinking about who we are in God and how we are living according to the image He created us in. Our redemption in Christ includes restoration of this level of spiritual sight and imagery.

The saying, the eyes are the windows to our souls, is so true. Matthew 6:22–23 says,

> The eye is the lamp of the body. You draw light into your body through your eyes, and light shines out to the world through your eyes. So if your eye is well and shows you what is true, then your whole body will be filled with light. But if your eye is clouded or evil, then your body will be filled with evil and dark clouds. And the darkness that takes over the body of a child of God who has gone astray—that is the deepest, darkest darkness there is.
>
> —The Voice

Our ability to see and be moved by image with our natural, mental, or spiritual eyes is God-given. We were created to recognize and understand image. Our visual sense was designed to draw us into the beauty of God. So rather than being afraid of our visual sense, what we need to do is be more critical of what we are looking at. We should be doing as Paul instructs in Philippians 4:8: "Whatsoever things are true, whatsoever things are honest, whatsoever things are just, whatsoever things are pure, whatsoever things are lovely, whatsoever things are of good report; if there be any virtue, and if there be any praise, think on these things."

Our senses are bombarded with information—sights, smells, touches, and more—every second. Our brain acts as a gatekeeper to all of it and throws out anything you do not need to help you deal with the things you are facing in the immediate moment.[7] Inhibitory neurons help us to "focus on what [we] want to see, rather than all there is to see."[8] This means we have the ability not to be swayed by every single image that pops up. We can actually train our eyes—spiritual and natural—to see what we want to see, what we need to see, and ultimately what God wants us to see.

Understanding the power of image is central to our being properly and prophetically connected to God. He instructs, warns, encourages, corrects, and inspires us through imagery. Job says that "in a dream, in a vision of the night, when deep sleep falleth upon men, in slumberings upon the bed; then he openeth the ears of men, and sealeth their instruction"

(Job 33:15–16). If we don't have vision, the Bible says, we perish (Prov. 29:18).

So when I tell you that we are about to embark on a journey to reclaim, reidentify, and restore our image of God, I believe that you can now quickly connect what I've been sharing about image, imagery, and imagination with the fact that distorted sight can keep us away from the superabundant life God has for us. What we see shapes us. The enemy knows this, and if he can get you to believe the images he puts in front of you, then he can keep you in turmoil and in a place of confusion. Not only that, he attempts to deceive you into believing your life has to be filled with stress, strife, and other toxic thoughts and behaviors. He knows that if he can come in and distort your imagery, everything in your life will be off kilter.

Many of us suffer from poor self-esteem, self-image, repeated cycles of spiritual and personal failure, the negative effects of dysfunctional relationships, and more because the image we pattern our lives after is skewed. We do not see the right image of God; therefore, we do not have the right image of ourselves. But what I hope to help you know with an unwavering faith is that God created you in His image. You are a copy of Him. You are called to be a habitation for His glory, presence, and beauty. You are called to be blessed, prosperous, confident, healthy, and whole. Yes, you!

No matter what you've done, what mistakes you've made,

God is passionately in love with you. He desires intimate, personal fellowship and relationship with you. He wants to bless you abundantly. He didn't just create born-again people in His image. All of mankind was created in the image and likeness of God. We need to get back to our original purpose, design, and pattern. Our vision needs to be restored so that we can begin to see ourselves the way that God sees us.

This book will help you get in position for vision restoration by reconnecting you with God's vision for your life. At the end of each chapter, I have prepared a set of questions arranged under the heading "Vision Quest," and a prayer called "Prayer to Bear His Image" that will help you on your path to becoming the true reflection of God He wants you to be and one that I believe you desire to be. You will want to get your own journal or notebook, set aside for this Image Bearers journey, to keep track of your answers and to take notes.

Encountering God Changes Everything

When we live with brokenness, we live beneath our position as image bearers. But when we encounter the living God, everything that has died within you will come alive. God desires that you would encounter Him. An encounter implies a confrontation. Encounter means to come face-to-face with someone or something. Encounter also means an unexpected meeting. It is in the nature of Jesus, the God-Man to encounter humanity—those whom He loves and died for.

Do you live with an expectation that you will encounter God? Are you daily anticipating divine intervention and answers to your prayers? When you encounter God, you encounter His power. We see this in Jesus' ministry as He healed and set free everyone who came to Him for healing.

God encounters should be a way of life, especially for believers. We have a relationship with God, made possible through Jesus, who has redeemed us. Through His blood, Jesus purchased and redeemed us, giving us access to our heavenly Father. We have become sons and daughters of Father God. It is through this same redemption that the image of God is restored in our lives.

If you know you are not seeing 20/20 through your spiritual eyes and are overdue for a spiritual vision prescription change, then I invite you on this journey to a restored position as God's image bearer.

Vision Quest

1. When is the last time you thought of God's vision for your life? What did you see? Name some tangible things like professional or calling, house, car, spouse, and the like. What about the intangibles—peace, love, fulfillment? Don't hold back. Write it all out in your journal.

2. In what ways has your vision been distorted from the 20/20 vision God had in mind for your life? What obstructions got in the way? Are there any areas where has your vision been corrected or sharpened? Name them.
3. Where do you see that your vision needs to be reset?
4. What needs to happen for you specifically to harness the power of your vision? What do you believe God wants you to see?
5. Encountering God in a real and authentic way changes everything and resets our vision for life. Do you live with an expectation that you will encounter God? In what ways can you think of that God has tried to encounter you? In thinking back over the last season or two of life, what divine interventions and answers to your prayers have demonstrated this?

Prayer to Bear His *Image*

Father, I lift up my hands to you in surrender. I confess that I have tried to live life as far as my eyes could see and that I've come to the end of that vision.

God, I repent for thinking that I could live according to my own limited views and understanding and ask that You will begin to show me where my image has been marred and broken. Show me places in my mental, spiritual, and emotional patterns and imagination that are off—those that don't reflect the kingdom.

I declare that this is a season of restoration. This is the season that You want to repair and restore my vision of who You are in me. I receive by faith the truth that I was created in Your image, that I bear Your divine and glorious image. Help me to walk in this truth.

Fine-tune my vision, O God. Fine-tune what I see. Let me set my sights on You. Let me behold Your beauty and inquire at Your temple all the days of my life that I may become more and more like You.

Restore my life. Redefine who I am. Let the power of Your image shine through me. Let me feel Your love and the warmth of Your embrace. Renew my mind's eye and let me see You as the loving Father You truly are.

In Jesus' name, I pray. Amen.

Chapter 2

AFTER HIS LIKENESS

And God said, Let us make man in our image, after our likeness: and let them have dominion over the fish of the sea, and over the fowl of the air, and over the cattle, and over all the earth….So God created man in his own image, in the image of God created he him; male and female created he them. And God blessed them, and God said unto them, Be fruitful, and multiply, and replenish the earth, and subdue it...And God saw every thing that he had made, and, behold, it was very good.
—Genesis 1:26–31

One definition of *image* is "exact likeness," "semblance," or resemblance of a person or object.[1] We can see this at work when we notice how one person may look strikingly like another. This happens mostly among family members and relatives. People may say something like, "Jonathan is the image of his father." I hear this, and it says to me that when that person looks at Jonathan, they see his dad. They see that he looks exactly like his father. This same thing can happen with a mother-daughter pair. Children can bear a very striking resemblance to their parents. Siblings can resemble each other as well. There can be a significant familial resemblance where it is easy to tell that people come from the same family by how they look, talk, or walk. By their image, we can associate people with their families.

In the family of God, there is an image. We are all called to "look" like Jesus and be like God. As we read above in Genesis 1:26, "God said, Let us make man in our image, after our likeness." In Leviticus 20:7 and 1 Peter 1:16, we hear from God again, when He commanded, "Be holy, as I am holy." Then in Matthew 5:48, Jesus reflected the words of His Father, saying, "Be ye therefore perfect, even as your Father which is in heaven is perfect."

God is calling us to reclaim His image, the image that gave Him the template by which He created us. We are to look like, resemble, depict, portray, represent, display, mirror, reflect, and put someone in the mind of God. When someone sees us, they should see God. Let's break this down more.

In the Bible's original Hebrew and Greek languages, the word *image* means slightly different things. In the Old Testament, the Hebrew word *tselem* is used for "image" in verses like Genesis 1:26 that we read above. It means "images (of tumours, mice, heathen gods)"; "image, likeness (of resemblance)"; "mere, empty, image, semblance (fig.)."[2] It can also mean "to shade" and can refer to "a phantom or illusion." Going a little further, we'll find that *image* can be a statue, profile, or copy. So, in essence, God was saying, "Let Us make man, and let him be a copy of who We are." Isn't that good? You are supposed to be a copy of the divine image and likeness of God.

In the New Testament the Greek word for "image" is *eikōn*. It's where our English word *icon* is derived. Merriam-Webster's Dictionary defines *icon* as "an object of uncritical devotion: idol"; "emblem, symbol"; "a usually pictorial representation: image."[3] In the Bible, we find *eikōn* used as the English word *image* in the following verses:

> For whom he did foreknow, he also did predestinate to be conformed to the *image* of his Son, that he might be the firstborn among many brethren.
>
> —ROMANS 8:29, EMPHASIS ADDED

> And as we have borne the *image* of the earthy, we shall also bear the *image* of the heavenly.
>
> —1 CORINTHIANS 15:49, EMPHASIS ADDED

> But we all, with open face beholding as in a glass the glory of the Lord, are changed into the same *image* from glory to glory, even as by the Spirit of the Lord.
>
> —2 CORINTHIANS 3:18, EMPHASIS ADDED

> And have put on the new man, which is renewed in knowledge after the *image* of him that created him.
>
> —COLOSSIANS 3:10, EMPHASIS ADDED

Though you can search other verses that use this same word, these few give us a picture of how God intended His image to reflect in our lives. His image reflects in our lives as "an image of the things (the heavenly things)"; "...the moral likeness of renewed men to God"; the image of the Son of God, into which true Christians are transformed, is likeness not only to the heavenly body, but also to the most holy and blessed state of mind, which Christ possesses."[4]

Like the breath of God breathed into man at creation, the image of God is not something that can be seen with the natural eye. It is a mental or spiritual picture of who we are to be. It is not something that is tangible. It is not actually present or anything we can touch. It is that which can only be perceived by the spirit of our minds—and we need our minds renewed in order to get back to living out the image of God.

> But the natural man receiveth not the things of the Spirit of God: for they are foolishness unto him: neither can he know them, because they are spiritually discerned.
>
> —1 CORINTHIANS 2:14

> Be renewed in the spirit of your mind.
>
> —EPHESIANS 4:23

When God created mankind, He created the perfect environment for us to encounter His full and unshielded presence.

Nothing was lacking. Adam and Eve were so secure in His love and provision that they did not have feelings of insecurity, exposure, and vulnerability to any kind of attack.

The Importance of a Restored Image

Understanding God, who He is, His nature, and His desire for mankind has been questioned and studied throughout time. Every generation seeks to understand God in some way. The pervasiveness of multiple spiritual belief systems is evidence of man's search for God. No matter what your belief system is or isn't, you are guaranteed to cry out to God at some time in your life, even if that point is while you are on your death bed. Just as a child longs for their mother who birthed them; we long for the God who created us. There is a sense of security that cannot be substituted when we can reestablish His image in our lives. Adam and Eve shattered the image, but we have a chance through Christ to have it made whole again.

It is so important for us to understand God's image, to know who God is and what He is really like, and not just how we have created Him to be in our minds. That image of Him won't do. We need to see through restored vision His true image.

YOU CHOOSE WHAT YOU SEE

We are God's greatest creation, and He made it so that we would also possess free will. Unlike animals who primarily function through instinct, mankind is above the beast of the field in every way. We have been endowed with the power of choice. Many times over, the Scriptures show how this is true:

> This day I call the heavens and the earth as witnesses against you that I have set before you life and death, blessings and curses. Now choose life, so that you and your children may live and that you may love the Lord your God, listen to his voice, and hold fast to him. For the Lord is your life, and he will give you many years in the land he swore to give to your fathers, Abraham, Isaac and Jacob.
>
> —DEUTERONOMY 30:19–20, NIV

A verse before we get here in Deuteronomy 30, God presents His people with the foreknowledge of what would happen if they did not choose life (v. 17). Being the good Father He is, He presented the full package—good and bad—and said, "Choose." In His love, He was also open with His desire for them to choose life, because "the Lord is your life" (v. 20). He wanted them to see that choosing the right way is the same as choosing Him. He was revealing His image to them.

In Joshua 24:15, we find the people of God at another crossroad of decision. Somehow, they had gotten away from the truth of God and began worshiping other gods. Joshua said to them, "If it seem evil unto you to serve the Lord, choose you this day whom ye will serve; whether the gods which your fathers served that were on the other side of the flood, or the gods of the Amorites, in whose land ye dwell: but as for me and my house, we will serve the Lord."

The people had begun to see God through a distorted lens and His image became tarnished to the point that they saw Him as evil and the idols good. As easy as it may feel to judge them, we don't need to look too far to see how—even in our society or our very own lives—God, His character, and His ways have come under harsh scrutiny to the extent people see Him and His Word as the enemy and everything else as perfectly plausible and acceptable.

This is indeed a sign of the times, where "people [love] the darkness rather than the light because their works [are] evil" (John 3:19). They "[change] the truth of God into a lie, and [worship] and [serve] the creature more than the Creator," and further they "they [do] not like to retain God in their knowledge" (Rom. 1:25, 28). Then Isaiah 5:20 says, "Woe unto them that call evil good, and good evil; that put darkness for light, and light for darkness; that put bitter for sweet, and sweet for bitter!"

Giving place to a distorted image of God and not cultivating what's necessary to retain the knowledge of the One

True God leads our lives into darkness, destruction, and death. This is why we must have our vision of God corrected.

THE ENEMY IS AFTER THE IMAGE

The enemy has been watching us since Creation. He is well aware that we were created in the image and likeness of God, and he wants to do everything in his power to make you lose sight of the image and in turn doubt who you are. We are not able to discern the fullness of who we are without knowing the fullness of who God is. There is an inseparable connection between our image and God's. Satan knows this and works overtime to sever the connection, and while he can't change the fact that we are created in the image of God, he can lead us to doubt what we've seen and heard of God, as he did with Eve in the garden. This doubt of the character and person of God leaves us naked and lost without a clear picture of our worth and identity. We find ourselves sitting in our situations not like the royalty we are but as second-class creations.

We begin to wrestle with feelings such as "God loves this other person more than He loves me? God always answers their prayers, but He never answers me. They are God's favorite, not me." When you feel like other people have greater favor, acceptance, or approval from God and you are the bad boy or girl, know this: your imagery is off, and it is time to adjust your view.

What the enemy does in this area of image is never about

one person. It's about a whole family of people. It's about generations of people. I know you didn't think he was just after you. Listen: He's after everybody you will ever influence, and to get to them, he first has to get you off the path. He has to get your focus off of God. He's looking for the access and entry points into our lives. He understands entry points and access points more than we do because we have become careless. One of the biggest points of entry is our image of God and ourselves.

Because of our falling to sin, we have a broken and shattered image at work in our lives. Have you ever looked in a mirror that's broken? You do not see a complete image. What you see are fracture lines. What you see, especially if some of the pieces have fallen out, you see pieces missing. The whole image is not there. The mirror is incapable of casting a full reflection of an image.

Having been in ministry as long as I have, I know the devastation the enemy brings to people. Some people have told me things like this: "I don't know what's wrong with me. I just can't seem to get it right. Everybody else seems to be able to live saved but not me. I don't know if I'm cursed. I don't know what's wrong with me. I just keep doing the same thing over and over, and I don't know why I do it."

Does this sound like you at some point in your walk with God?

The more you respond to the devil's smoke-and-mirrors tricks, the farther he drags you into a seeming point of no return, where your emotions and everything else become so dull that you don't even respond to the wooing of God.

CHOOSE TO SEE GOD AS LIFE

Though I am going to discuss this next point more fully in the next chapter, I want to introduce it here as I hope to begin to help you change your mental picture. In John 10:10, Jesus said, "The thief cometh not, but for to steal, and to kill, and to destroy: I am come that they might have life, and that they might have it more abundantly."

This word *destroy* doesn't just mean to crumple; it means to totally annihilate, it means to utterly destroy, it means to perish, it means to lose or die. It's to cease; it's to separate. It means a cessation, a reversal.

As I said above, the enemy is after the image.

Now, let me define one more word—*life*. In this scripture, that word is the Greek word *zoe*,[5] which is, as I take it to mean, the God kind of life. But more literally, it means "the absolute fulness of life, both essential and ethical, which belongs to God."[6]

And this is the very thing the enemy has come to attack in you, to blow smoke in your eyes, to blur and distort your vision of God, to confuse your mind, and to bring you to a place where you begin to feel helpless and hopeless as if there is no way out for you. He wants you to believe you have no right to the "absolute fulness of life" in God. But when you can't see God, this is your reality. You will only feel as if He has forsaken you.

However, this is the distortion God is trying to break through. From ancient times until now His declaration remains the same: "I am come that you might have life, and that you might have it abundantly." What this word *abundantly* means here is superabundance. This level of abundance that Jesus is speaking of here is excessive. It's overflowing. It means to have a surplus, to have over and above, and more than enough. It's about being profusely, extraordinarily blessed.[7]

He is saying to you today, "This is how much of my life I want you to have. I want you to be oozing with my life."

Now here is the beginning for how you can align yourself to partake in this superabundant life: you must yield yourself over to God. The more you give yourself to God, the more He gives Himself to you. The more you submit yourself to Him, the more of Him you see manifested in you.

The enemy comes to totally annihilate the God kind of life that is supposed to be flowing in you. As Jesus said, "Out of [your] belly shall flow rivers of living water" (John 7:38). But Kleptes (the Greek word for "thief,"[8]) says, "I come to block up the flow of living water. I can't kill it, because it comes from God, but what I'm going to do is try to block it up, so nothing flows out of that person."

Satan has an idea about your destiny. He has an idea about how powerful you are and what you will bring from heaven into the earth realm. The Bible says that he knows his time to deceive, steal, kill, and destroy is short (see Revelation 12:12). He knows that his time to capture the vision of man is drawing to a close, so he is working overtime. But we have a God who says that soon My justice will roll like a river and judgment will surely come. Vengeance is mine. Soon, I will repay." It's important for us to make it known now what we choose to see. God will work to correct our vision. Just what will we choose to set our eyes on?

In the next chapter, we are going to look at how the enemy works to recast the image of God. This is important to know as we come into agreement with God in our process of restoring His image in our lives. We need not be ignorant of the devil schemes.

Vision Quest

1. What is your vision of God? How do you see Him? Honestly assess what characteristics of His you have experienced in your life? This does not need to be what someone else says you should see. What have you believed and seen of Him in connection with you and your life? Now answer each of these questions for the other Persons of the godhead:

    a. Holy Spirit

    b. The Son, Jesus

2. Based on the Scriptures and teaching in chapter 2—and

perhaps the verses and lessons you've been taught—how does your vision of God agree with the Word of God, the Bible? How is it different?

3. Now what about you? How do your behaviors and beliefs reflect who God is? How does your life demonstrate God's goodness?
4. Write out a thank-you note to God for where things in your life connect between His character and goodness.
5. Make a list identifying the gaps between how you see God and what His Word says and the gaps between His goodness and how your life demonstrates it. Begin to pray for new vision on how those areas can come into alignment with Him.

Prayer to Bear His *Image*

Father, I thank You that I have been fearfully and wonderfully made in your image. Thank You for coming down into the earth, bending down over me, and fashioning me for Your glory. I am in awe of Your works.

This is the very divine thing that the enemy has come into my life to steal, kill, and destroy, but I rebuke the enemy. I am not ignorant of His devices. So, Father, I ask that You will set up a standard against Him, O God. Shield me from the destroyer and teach my hands to war that I may be strong in the evil day and fight the good fight of faith.

Lord, I also repent for the doors I have opened that have allowed the thief access to my life. I pray even now that those doors be shut and that everything that's been stolen be returned sevenfold. Let my life come back into alignment with You. Let my life reflect Your goodness. Let me live in the light of Your glory forever.

In Jesus' name, I pray. Amen

Chapter 3

IMAGE ROBBER

The thief cometh not, but for to steal, and to kill, and to destroy: I am come that they might have life, and that they might have it more abundantly.
—John 10:10

In reexamining this popular verse, the first thing God revealed to me is that Jesus says, "The thief," and then he says, "He steals." The words *thief* and *steal* come from the same Greek word, *klepto,* which is where we get the word *kleptomaniac.*[1] I'm sure you are familiar with this term. So, when we are talking about the enemy, we are talking about a kleptomaniac or klepto, as we sometimes say. He is an "embezzler," "pilferer"; one who steals, commits theft, or takes away by stealth.[2]

When you understand the nature of "kleptomania," you will understand that God, through His Word, is trying to tell us that Satan has "a persistent neurotic impulse to steal especially without economic motive."[3] In other words, like all kleptomaniacs, he doesn't even need what he steals. He steals because he wants to steal, because he can steal, and to see if he can get away with it. He steals also because He hates God and anything that looks like God. He steals so that the glory of God can't be seen in the lives of who God created. He steals so that he can make God a liar. He steals so that instead of casting him out of our lives, we blame God for the sin and mess in our lives. He steals from us to make us think God hates us. He steals so that we won't have faith to believe that we are to live an abundant life. He steals, and he steals everything and anything—especially the true image of a loving God, who gave up everything for us so that we could access everything in Him.

But he doesn't stop at stealing. He also kills. The word *kill* in Greek is the word *thyo,* which means "to slay"; "to rush (breathe hard...)." The next two words are, I think, the most powerful—"blow," "smoke." *To kill* can be translated to mean "to blow" or "smoke."[4]

Have you ever seen a magic show? The magician uses smoke to create an illusion of something that is actually not there and to draw your attention to something else. And that's what the enemy does: when he comes to destroy your image of God or any other good and holy thing God set before you, the enemy blows smoke in front of your spiritual eyes so that you don't see what actually just took place.

This diversion is often referred to as "smoke and mirrors," a manipulation magicians, performers, or, in our case, the enemy uses to control what is visible to you, the viewer. What is seen is not really the way it is; it's the way the enemy wants you to think it is. What's happening is not really what's happened; it's what he wants you to think just happened. What you may be feeling about the way God feels about you is not the truth of how God feels, but it's what the enemy is leading you to believe by what he is making visible through his tricks and illusions.

The other parts of this translation of "to kill" leads us to familiar words such as *slay* and *slaughter*.[5] He comes to slay and slaughter our image of God. He comes to slay and slaughter our future in God that is filled with hope and prosperity. He comes to slay and slaughter dreams and destinies; purposes, provision, and peace; and salvation and healing.

What's even more interesting is that the word *sacrifice* also appears in the translation.[6] What do the enemy's snares and tactics lead us to sacrifice? What is on his idolatrous altar to be slaughtered that is keeping us from an abundant life? What are we sacrificing the longer we live with a shattered image of God? I challenge you to submit these questions to the Lord in prayer, hear what He tells you, and begin to speak life to those dead things that they may live again.

When you think of the word *destroy*, I am trusting you get the full idea of what this means, that you don't get an image of crumpled paper or something. Please know this: the enemy seeks to obliterate the plan of God in your life. I can't say this enough: the devil hates God and all those who look like Him. By any means necessary, he works to keep you from living according to the declaration Christ makes in the second part of this verse—"I am come that they might have life, and that they might have it more abundantly."

Satan, therefore, comes not to wrinkle, ball up, tear, or beat up. He comes to destroy, "to put out of the way entirely, abolish, put an end to ruin", to "render useless" the thing that gives you hope, the thing that drives you to sit at the throne of God, gazing at His beauty, that image that by beholding it, you become changed. No, the devil does not come to crumple or crush. For as Paul says, "We are troubled on every side, yet not distressed; we are perplexed, but not in despair; persecuted, but not forsaken; cast down, but not destroyed" (1 Cor. 4:8–9). In essence, Paul was saying, "Look, you can throw me down, but I'm not destroyed. I can come back from this. I can get back up. I might be down, but I'm not out." Look at this too in verse 10: "Always bearing about in the body the dying of the Lord Jesus, that the life also of Jesus might be made manifest in our body." He kept within his heart and mind the image of the crucified Christ, which gave him hope that he might manifest the abundant life in Christ. What you see makes a big difference in how you live.

RECASTING THE IMAGE

In returning to the Creation story, let's look at Genesis 3:1: "Now, the serpent was more subtle and crafty than any living creature of the field which the Lord God had made. And he, Satan, said to the woman, 'Can it really be that God has said you should not eat from every tree of the garden?'" (AMP).

Hearing it in our ears, in today's language, it might sound like this: "Is that really true? I can't believe that's what God said to you. Why would He say that? Are you sure that, in all this paradise, He would want to limit you like that? I can't believe He would say that to you. I can't believe He played you like that. I can't believe He put you in this place, with all this provision, and then He's going to try to put you on lockdown."

He is a master at inching us further and further away from God's intent and the heart of God's instructions for living the superabundant life. He is a roaring lion who devours us by luring us into the trap of lies and deceit. He gets us ready for the kill by distorting our image of God.

He does not want you to see God as a loving father. He does not want you to see that God accepts you unconditionally. He does not want you to see that God has your best interests at heart. He does not want you to believe that you can live a godly quality of life on Earth. Instead, He wants you to believe that resting in the peace, safety, and provision of God is not for you, that somehow God is cheating you out of a fun, prosperous, and exciting life. He does not want you to believe that you can live in the place of God's rest. He works hard to shatter our image of God, because if we really see who God is, then we can more accurately see ourselves.

When I think about this, I can't help but see the images that we stereotypically relate to psychiatrists. You know what I'm referring to? The inkblot images, where the patient is asked to tell the doctor what they see. How they answer helps the doctor know what their emotional state is. The inkblot may not be an actual image; it could be anything. The patient may say, "I see a cow." In another session, another patient may say, "I see a knife." In yet another, one may say, "I see a whole room full of people dead." Each of these responses tells the psychiatrist something about this person's state of mind or focus. With this last response, it may not be too hard to know that this patient has murder on their mind. I'll repeat it again, what we see makes a big difference in how we live.

The Thief Comes In

Now that he's recast God's image—His words and intention, His instruction, character, and heart—the enemy can now just come in and take whatever he wants. Look at it like this: the image of God is like a fine art piece. If we don't understand the value of the art, we may just think it's an old, ugly thing. Satan has led us to devalue the image of God in much the same way. We don't see its truth, its power, or that our identity is cast from it. We just see it as outdated and restrictive. Once we've gotten this perspective, we're set up for easy pickings. The enemy has cased our valuables. He's gotten many of us to the point that we don't even lock them up anymore.

Your life is set up like a gated community, and the thief has discovered that you have priceless treasures in your house.

These priceless treasures are your gifts, calling, purpose, and destiny. These things are of no use for the thief—remember he's a klepto. Your kingdom possessions are valuable in part because, when you activate them, they lead you toward living the life that Christ died for you to have. If he can steal those, He can steal everything.

To get in at just the right moment, a thief begins to watch how you come and go. He starts to check out your security system. He watches all of your patterns. He looks for any area of vulnerability in your life so that he can gain access to your valuables. This is the level of cunning a natural thief has, so imagine how much Satan, an ancient spirit, has. He is able to look at you from a generational dimension to learn how to gain access into your family line. Doing this, he can distort the image of God not just in the life of one individual but in the lives of generations to come.

He wants to make it so that it is not only you who lives a broken and separated life. His level of destruction is aimed at all that concerns you. He destroys to bring people and things to a place where they think God can never use them again.

And here's where I want to make a special point to you if you've been dealing with cycles of perpetual backsliding. To break out of your situation and return to a life of stability and peace, you need to pray against some unseen things, some roots, and some generational curses that have been set in motion before you were born. You may be up against things like addiction and personality issues like anger, bitterness, and self-pity for which you did not necessarily open the door. You keep backsliding and doing what you're doing because the enemy has been after your image of God for a long time. He wants to bring you to a place of no return. You may not be able to see Him clearly now, but by God's power, the message I am sharing in this book will set you free. Your vision will be restored. And you will begin to walk a stable and established life no matter if you are the first in your family to do so. Let that faith and hope arise in you today, in Jesus' name.

THE ENEMY STRIKES HARD

Over the years, I've begun to see a pattern in how the enemy alters God's image and how we give in to his lies, inch by inch. We slowly allow the enemy in to steal, kill, and destroy. Let's take a look at some of his key moves in strategic areas of our lives.

- Sexual purity: The enemy says, "I can't really believe God expects you to be single, live saved, and not indulge yourself sexually. Why would He have created you with these desires if He didn't want you to enjoy yourself just once?"
- Financial giving and stewardship: When it's time to give, the enemy says, "I cannot believe

God expects you not to have enough money. Doesn't He understand you're living in hard times, that you don't make enough money? I don't think it's fair He expects you to pay your tithes in the situation you're in, do you? What kind of God would force someone to live like that?

- Marriage troubles/relationship: The enemy says, "I can't really believe God expects for you to love your wife, as Christ loved the church. After all, she isn't an easy person to love. She's boring, dumb, and stupid. I can't believe He expects you to love that woman in spite of all the flaws she has. I can't believe God expects for you to love that woman who won't even submit to you. I mean, how can you really love a person like that?"

- Church attendance: "Does God really expect you to attend church on a regular basis? Does He not see these gas prices? Doesn't He know you're busy?"

- Living holy and righteous: "I can't believe God expects you to do all these kinds of things. He should know you're only human."

- Self-control and obedience: "I cannot believe God puts those kinds of limitations and restrictions on you. After all, they provoked you. You have a right to respond using colorful language. They have been gossiping about you and it's time you spoke up for yourself.
- Fasting and prayer: "I can't believe the church leaders expect you to turn your plate down and fast and be hungry. Don't they know your blood sugar will drop and you might faint?" "I can't believe that they expect for you to get up out of bed early in the morning to pray. Won't it have the same effect if you pray on your lunch hour instead?"
- Kindness: "Did they just ask you for a ride? When is the last time anyone in this church has done anything for you? You get what you give out right? They haven't given a thing to you. Why should you do something for them? I can't believe they expect you to show—what are they calling it now—brotherly kindness? God will surely understand that you are just abiding by the law of sowing and reaping. After all, it's your car."

He comes and distorts the image and blows it way out of proportion. Sometimes he uses people to do it—people who have a voice or influence. They become his oracles. Eve became this for Adam. The devil used the influence Eve had over Adam's life to cause all of mankind to fall. See, Satan is not just after you. He's after everyone who is or will be connected to you.

Your husband, your wife, your pastor, your father or mother, your friend, the people you go to church with, and even those in your prayer group can be used by the enemy to steal your most valuable spiritual assets. Without their being aware, Satan can use their words to cause you to doubt what you know about what God said and who He is in your life. This is why our own vision must be corrected and sharpened.

Eve probably thought she was bringing Adam a good thing. I'm sure she had brought him fruit before. Tasting its sweetness and feeling no ill effects, she offered it in kindness to her husband. Trusting the woman God gave him, he ate it and immediately they were naked and vulnerable. (See Genesis 3:6–7.)

There's only so much other people will know about what God told you and what you need to do to remain faithful and obedient to Him. When we trust other voices more than we trust God, we are at risk for others to control our lives in ungodly ways. Ungodly voices seek to control every area of our lives—what to wear, what music is OK for us, and what places are safe for our leisure and entertainment. They reinterpret the word of the Lord over our lives to fit what they think we should be allowed to do from one moment to the next. And many of them may be well meaning. However, they can tell you what they think and know based on their walk and how they see God, but you must be firm in God's revealed image to you. The enemy counts on our reliance on second-hand imagery, distorted views, and misguided ideologies. And there are times when we follow these images that we are led directly into a trap.

We'll hear the enemy in our ear, saying, "Can it really be? Did He really say that? Is that what He really expects? It can't really be stealing if the cashier gave you too much change back. That's a blessing from the Lord. He knows how tight things have been for you lately. I can't believe God wants you to return the money." When this happens, you need to shut him up and tune into your spirit man. You need to be questioning yourself: "If God is giving this money to me as a blessing, why is my heart beating so fast? Why am I in flight mode? Why am I walking out of the store three times faster than normal?" If you did go forward with the money, ask yourself, "Why do I not want to go back into that store?" We have the Holy Spirit who gives us checks when we are about to make a wrong decision and even after the bad decision was made. Yet, who are we choosing to see?

Another image-reflecting scenario that's popular: "Is it really wrong that you bought that outfit, which you really couldn't afford, wore it one time, and returned it? I mean, you tucked the tags on the inside, made sure to keep the receipt, and wore it to the event, intending to return it. They don't know if it was the wrong size or that you might not have liked it. God should understand."

Your Part in the Enemy's Recasting

There are so many other ways the enemy comes alongside us and breaks another piece of the mirror through which we see God. He does it through keeping us isolated from kingdom-minded believers, fathers and mothers who are strong in the faith who will help us remain accountable to the word of the Lord spoken over our life. They help you to keep your eyes on the image of God He showed you those many years ago. Instead, the enemy has you believing you don't really need a true Bible-believing, strong-in-the-prophetic church.

Being an island unto yourself is not OK. Not having anyone to call and pray with you is not OK. Not having accountability is not OK. It's not OK that you don't want anyone talking to you. Satan will come right alongside you with his, "Can it really be that we need to be part of a covenantal community? Can it be that we need to be connected to each other? Can it be that we need to receive the ministry of mothers and fathers who are in the house of God? Can it be that we should operate with honesty and with integrity?

Can it be that we should not let our children hear us gossip about the church?" Yes, it can be, and it is so. It is absolutely the heart of God that you remain connected to Him and His body, that you display His fruit, that you walk righteously, that you speak the truth in love. We must seek after and trust in the unadulterated image of God—His glory, His holiness, His righteousness, and His love for us. Anything less and our view of God gets distorted, and we waver with feelings of insecurity and unbelief.

Hear me when I say this: your trust in God cannot be destroyed without your coming into agreement with the enemy's lies.

Eve's trust in God could not be destroyed without her participation. The imagery of God in us cannot be stifled without our involvement. We have to come into agreement with the enemy. When he says God loves someone else more than He loves you, you essentially have to nod your head and say, "You're right, devil."

When he says, "If God loved you all that much, He wouldn't let this infirmity happen to you," then you've got to nod your head and say, "You know, you're right, devil."

"And if God loved you like that, He would have healed you the first time you asked Him," and you keep coming in agreement, saying, "You know what, you're right, devil."

The next thing you won't even realize is that he came in a destroyed the image of God you once set your gaze upon. Now you're mad at God, and every time you hear somebody's testimony, instead of your faith and expectation rising for your own healing, instead of rejoicing with them, you're upset. Why? Because you have participated with the enemy for the creation of wrong imagery in your mind.

It is not appealing to realize that you basically partnered with the enemy in the orchestration of your demise but that is exactly what self-sabotage is, or if I may use a heavier term here—self-mutilation. We have exercised our right to choose, and we have chosen Satan's mutilated image of God. As His image in our eyes is marred and mutilated—He's unloving, angry, and ready to punish—we see ourselves as shameful, guilty, and unloveable, so we run to all kinds of "fig leaves"—addiction, illegal sex, pride, attention-seeking, and other things—to cover up the shame and ugliness we see in ourselves.

What a sad place to be. And because of this, Adam and Eve were terrified when they heard God call to them. Their image of Him was the direct cause for that fear. Satan experienced a momentary victory, but just as God had a plan then, He has a plan today to help you see Him for who He is so that you will live in peace and security. He has the best in mind for you.

1. What has the enemy's snares and tactics led you to sacrifice? What have you laid on his idolatrous altar that is

keeping you from an abundant life? What is at stake for you?

2. What power can the image of the crucified Christ have in your life?
3. In what ways have you fallen for the enemy's smoke and mirror's tricks?
4. In what ways have you recasted God's image?
5. Has this recasting caused you to be angry with God? If so, how has this anger with God manifested in your life? This may not be an easy thing to admit. But think deeply and pray that your eyes may be opened in this area. What remains in the dark must come to light if your vision is to be restored to 20/20.

PRAYER TO BEAR HIS *Image*

God, this is hard, but I am grateful for Your grace in allowing me to see the ways I have been living with the wrong image of You in my view. Thank You for not leaving me even in the times when I saw You as my enemy. Please forgive me for falling for the enemy's tricks—his smoke and mirrors. I am sorry for doubting Your word over my life, Your hand of direction, warning, and even correction. You are a good Father.

Now please open my eyes to the recasted image of You that has been leading my life down the path of darkness, sin, and shame. Show me where I have fallen for the enemy's smoke and mirrors. Show me where I have run and hidden from You.

Lord, I do not want to continue sacrificing the abundant life You have for me. I desire to live out the image You have for my life. Teach me. Forgive me. Restore me.

In Jesus' name, amen.

Chapter 4

OUT OF FOCUS

The eyes of them both were opened, and they knew that they were naked.
—Genesis 3:7

For now we see through a glass, darkly; but then face to face: now I know in part; but then shall I know even as also I am known.
—1 Corinthians 13:12

Just after creation and before their fall, Adam and Eve's image was so tuned to God that they did not know they lacked anything. This is the spiritual place where God wants us to dwell, and we are there when we see Him through the right lens. When we see Him as all-sufficient, Jehovah Jireh, we will see ourselves as lacking no good thing. God created Adam and Eve without natural or physical clothes. They didn't need them. They were naked but shielded and clothed in the glory of God. They had no idea it needed to be any other way. But then they committed a transgression.

They ate the fruit from the Tree of the Knowledge of Good and Evil and "the eyes of them both were opened."

The Bible says they heard the voice of God as He walked in the garden in the evening (v. 8). They knew that this was the time they would usually go and welcome fellowship with God, but something had happened to them. A new image had been created—an image that left them feeling poor and empty.

When you are really focused on the true image of God, you really don't pay a lot of attention to what you don't have, because you are in the place of worship. God has your attention, and you know He has your best interest at heart. You can see that everything you need He will supply. Being in tune with the image of God is what helps you walk by faith and not by sight. You will see limitations as opportunities for God to manifest His will and power in your life. Instead of responding the way Adam and Eve did, you will instead think, "What? Naked? What is naked? Am I naked? God didn't tell me I was naked." That's childlike dependence on who God says you are in Him. It helps you to keep moving despite the enemy's attempt to shatter your image.

While they were in a place of transgression, Adam and Eve began to focus on themselves instead of God, and our focus has been inward ever since. We have stopped looking at Him, and now we look at ourselves. We are self-focused and not God focused because the image that motivates us has changed from one of godliness, glory, and perfection to one that is tainted and temporal. Our image has been tampered with.

The Bible says, in 2 Corinthians 3:18: "But we all, with open face beholding as in a glass the glory of the Lord, are changed into the same image from glory to glory, even as by the Spirit of the Lord." In the simplest terms, I've heard it said that by beholding anything long enough, we become changed or influenced by that thing. This is why, as kingdom people, our image of God is so important for us as we seek to live according to His plan for our lives.

The reason you are living a life that is falling short or less than abundant is because your focus is off. You know why you don't want to really live a life committed to God? Because you're looking at yourself. You are considering what you want and not what God wants for you.

Some believers are still wrestling with whether God really said fornication or adultery is wrong. They are wondering if the lack of control over what they put in their body is really all that bad, or if idolatry in the form of addiction is really what God wants them to stay away from. Yes, He did say it. Both the fruit that comes from a life lived in His Spirit and the works that come from a life that does not are listed in Galatians 5:19–25.

When our focus becomes inward, we begin to see all of the things we don't have. We start looking at our level of intelligence. We start looking at our physical features. We start looking at other people's families. We start looking at other people's cars. We start looking at their wardrobe. We start looking at all of the natural things, and we begin to look within ourselves, and say, "Something must be wrong with me because I don't have these things."

Instead of acknowledging that Adam could name every animal, that he was smart enough to know the differences in animals, plants and other aspects of creation, that he recognized woman when he saw her, they saw that they were naked, lacking clothes. Adam had the intelligence to name every animal, but how did he not have the intelligence to know that hiding in the bushes with some fig leaves was not going to cover them and hide them from God? What happened there? What was the disconnect? His focus was off. That's what caused him to see so blindly. When Adam's imagery changed, it affected his level of intelligence.

UNWRAP YOUR FIG LEAVES

Guilt, shame, and condemnation soon followed their lowered mental state, and rather than confess their sin, they went searching for a false covering to hide themselves. We've been using false coverings ever since. Here are some examples of our modern-day fig leaves.

Excessive outward adornment

Perhaps you will recognize your own fig leaves in these examples. Women sometimes wear excessive amounts of makeup trying to cover up the flaws we think we see in our faces. Unnatural hair lengths, colors, and textures can communicate a level of insecurity we have with our appearances. Some women—and some men, for that matter—are outlandish in their dress. These can be fig leaves—false coverings. We want to hide our brokenness from others and sometimes from God himself by putting on false exteriors to keep the truth from being revealed. We paint false images on the outside that say, "I'm the sunshine girl," but on the inside, we are weeping. We are projecting false imagery. We're using a false cover.

We can see this in men as well with addictions to working out, wearing only expensive clothes and accessories, never wanting a hairline edge out of place, and buying various kinds of expensive status symbols.

Now please understand that I am not making a sweeping generalization about makeup, dress, or hairstyle. Many women just love beautiful things that enhance or reflect the beauty that is already inside them. And there are men who are good stewards of their health and bodies and see themselves as the temple of God. These men and women are confident, creative, and expressive in how they present themselves. Some of their self-care and grooming methods are reflections of the beauty and glory of God because they are first filled with love, humility, and kindness.

In pointing out how some people are excessive and even obsessed with their outward appearance, I hope to convey that our motivations are direct reflections of the image we've focused in on. Is this image one of insecurity, where we use exterior things to mask our vulnerabilities? Or, is it that we feel loved and beautiful on the inside so what we wear on the outside is a reflection of the glorious image of God in us? These are image matters that I want to bring to the surface so that our focus may be realigned. There can be no vision correction without first diagnosing where things are wrong.

Loud talking and bragging

Here's another example of a false covering. Have you ever been in a room with a person who speaks very loudly, as if what they have to say is more important than what anyone else has to say and all eyes need to be on them? This same type of person may even invent happenings and events in their lives just to get the oohs, ahs, and wows. When you pull back all of their false covering, all you see is a small, emotional, and perhaps rejected person. They used the false covering of loudness and boasting to try to give the impression of confidence and strength. They hope that those things will speak louder for them than the truth of their failures and weaknesses.

Remember how the characters in the *Wizard of Oz* went through all that drama to see the Wizard.[1] Yet, after all the tests, trials, and tribulations they went through to get there, they pulled back the curtain, and there's just this little person about two feet tall. This is the truth of what it's like when we remove the fig leaves—a spiritually, emotionally, and mentally feeble person is revealed.

Overachievement and Perfectionism

Have you ever heard of overachievement? Of course, you have. Maybe you struggle with it yourself. Overachieving is in many ways a false covering for inadequacy. Overachievers need to be better or smarter than everybody. Some of them are relentlessly competitive with themselves. Some overachieving behavior is projected onto someone else. I have seen some parents do this with their children. Sometimes putting pressure on them to earn a 4.0 GPA each semester. When we do not give our children unconditional love and acceptance God gives us, we are setting them up to be professional false-covering, fig-leaf clothing designers. Maybe we are like this because of unresolved childhood trauma. But this is why we must have a vision correction.

Parents are the key projectors of the image of God in their children's lives. We need to be able to look at our children through eyes of love. We need to recognize the cognitive and academic ability of our children and try not to push them into being Einsteins when they are uniquely who God made them to be—Jessica, Tyrone, Matthew, or Latasha. There's so much hurt we cause when we make them feel like we don't love them if they aren't outstanding according to some ungodly image.

Some people are perfectionists with many things. One is housekeeping. Their clean house is a false covering because it helps them project an image they want other people to see of them while they hide their true selves.

Aggression, humor, silence, and other false coverings

Others use aggression as a false covering because they don't want people to know how afraid they are. Outside of genuine good-naturedness and sincere expressions of extroversion, there are some who use humor to cover up the fact that they are weeping on the inside. Then there's silence. For some it's an authentic personality trait—they are thinkers. For others, they are afraid to be heard because they fear their ideas or input will be rejected or that they will reveal how much they don't know. So they just don't talk.

Religion and various forms of idolatry can also be used as a false cover for heart issues. If we let our flesh have its way, pride would rise up and cause us all to cover what God needs to heal, restore, and redeem. At our core, we really don't want people to know the weak or dark parts of who we are, so we hide just like our first parents did.

Trust God with your fig leaves

The big problem with our fig leaves is that we're using a natural thing to cover ourselves and to gain acceptance from a source other than God. But here's the truth: When I'm feeling broken, having what I think is the worst day of my life, when I've been angry all day long, or whatever is going on in my life, I can present myself to God just like that. I don't have to try and fix or cover myself before I go before His throne. Neither you nor I need to think that we have to try and change ourselves before we come to God. The Bible says that we can come boldly before the throne of God to find help in our time of need (Heb. 4:16). Psalm 103: 14 says, "For he knoweth our frame; he remembereth that we are dust." Therefore, He says, "I already know you're broken. Just come to me, and I'll do the changing."

The fig leaves and all their ungodly results are reflective of our attempts to change ourselves. They are manmade solutions to God-size problems. Fig leaves only cover the wound. Setting ourselves under the light of God's image routs out the weaknesses, lack, and insecurity, as He clothes us in His glory, and brings us to complete healing and restoration.

Don't Be a Shallow Hal

The enemy works to keep us from complete healing and restoration. As long as he can keep us believing that our fig leaves are actually doing a good job of covering us, we will work hard to keep up the false image. Consider the person who suffers from anorexia. The eating disorder has emotional roots, but the spiritual root of it is based on wrong imagery. When the sufferer goes to the mirror, they see a very overweight person, though, many times, they are adults weighing under one hundred pounds. They are virtually dying, as they are undernourished and misinformed about their true image. Intervention after intervention, they cannot see the truth and will not eat. Sadly, their image is distorted.

The movie *Shallow Hal* is all about imagery, isn't it?[2] The main character, Hal, is a vain guy—a pig, really. He is so arrogant that he only pursues beautiful women, but something happens to him where he starts seeing women who are very overweight as if they are petite and svelte. His imagery had been altered, and no matter how much his friends balked at his new plus-size love interest or how much they told him she was overweight, he did not see her that way. In some ways, this can be seen as an object lesson for the main character, but for our purposes, this is a clear example of someone with impaired vision.

As we can see, wrong imagery carries out into everyday life. Our imagery of God can be skewed to the point of affecting some of our most important relationships. One of these relationships is the one we have with our earthly fathers. God is often likened to a father. We pray to Him as Father (Matt. 6:9). He blesses us and gives us gifts like a father (Matt. 6:4; 7:11). He disciplines us like a father (Heb. 12:6). He lavishes love on us like a father (1 John 3:1). If we had an abusive father, however, then it is hard for us to begin to receive God's love, because our image of a Father is of someone who is abusive. If we grew up without a father, then we may believe that God is distant or that He may abandon us.

Additional daddy issues surface in other areas of our lives, especially when we consider our need for male affirmation. There's nothing wrong with it as it is something God created in us to help us stay connected to Him and in healthy relationships with our families of origin. Some of these daddy issues play out in people's lives in the form of sexual promiscuity. We sometimes see this manifest in the lives of young girls who are always seeking attention from boys. Some of them begin sleeping around at young ages because they are so desperate to fill their need for love and approval. Though they are sometimes unaware, their behavior is motivated by a shattered image of what love is. This false image of love, generated by issues of abandonment and rejection, is actually lust, and their ability to draw attention from boys becomes their fig leaves. They bear the abuse and lies from men all for the momentary and false image of being desired. Ultimately, what they are aiming for is to be loved, affirmed, and to be somebody's princess. They want and need their loving image of God restored.

Misinformation Leads to Distrust, Which Leads to Wrong Imagery

Getting back to our lead story, we know that Satan worked hard to change how Adam and Eve saw God. He started with causing Eve to question if she even heard God correctly. And then after their transgression, their focus shifted from God to themselves. But there's another point I want to extrapolate from the serpent and Eve's exchange. Let's go back there now.

In Genesis 3:2, it says, "The woman said to the serpent, 'We can eat of the trees, from the fruit of the garden, except the fruit from the tree which is in the middle of the garden. God has said, 'You should not eat of it, neither shall you touch it, lest you die.'"

I imagine that, to the serpent, Eve must have seemed unsure about what she thought God had said. He took her statement and reframed it as a question as if she was asking for clarity on what she heard from God. Satan milked the opportunity, casting doubt and fear.

Because Eve went to the wrong source for confirmation, she positioned herself to receive the wrong information. The wrong source yields wrong information. When we are operating from a place of misinformation, misinformation always takes us in the wrong direction. You cannot make the right decisions based on the wrong information.

The enemy countered her newness in God with an attack on her view of God's trustworthiness. He does the same with us. He does not want us to trust God. Trust is the foundation for every healthy relationship. Satan wants to destroy that very thing—your relationship with God.

He does not want you to yield yourself to God totally. He does not want you to have kingdom imagery in your mind. He wants to sever your lifeline to God's image so that you do not fulfill the purposes of God for your life.

The Danger of Thinking Independently

As we saw played out in the first part of this chapter, part of Satan's first work was to make Eve feel like she could not trust God to tell her the truth. And because she couldn't trust God to tell her the truth, she then had to find the truth for herself, which meant she had to act independently of God. After all, she couldn't trust Him to tell her the truth.

I imagine, as other scholars, preachers, and theologians have, that Adam was walking around talking to God. Maybe he was out naming more plants and animals and learning how to care for them. Whatever he may have been doing, the thought has been that he wasn't talking to Eve very much. If he had been, she probably wouldn't have been speaking to the serpent. The Bible doesn't let us know what Adam was doing at the time Eve was tempted, but what we do get a sense for is that Eve was out on her own. She had moved from a place of dependence to a place of independence.

It may seem admirable to be known as an independent thinker. Society encourages it. In most cases, it is a good thing in terms of not allowing yourself to be controlled by people or situations. Yet, to truly be wise in your thinking, your mind must be renewed and submitted to the counsel of God and those He positions in our life for accountability and growth. Any thinking done independently from God and His will for your life will lead to death and destruction.

Get Your Focus Back

God has made available to you kingdom resources capable of encouraging and strengthening you during difficult times. It is important to develop kingdom relationships with other likeminded believers. Some of these kingdom resources might be your pastor and other leaders in your church. Pray and ask the Holy Spirit to lead you to those who will give you wise counsel and pray with and for you as you seek wholeness. Seek first the counsel of God and stay in communion with Him allowing His direction to those who have capacity and maturity to direct you.

Godly counsel that helps shift your focus back to God is not overbearing, where you tell the person every detail of your life and ask for their counsel for every little thing you do. But when you feel you've lost your way, they can be there to point you back to God and say, "What did God tell you about your future? Who does He say you are in His word? What did God reveal to you about buying that home, car, etc.?" Trust God to connect you with those who can provide godly counsel and accountability for your life.

Leaning on the spiritual gifts and ministry offices present in the body of Christ is a great way to keep your eyes on the true image of God. Never forsaking the corporate assembly, never taking your communion with God for granted, your gaze will be fixed on the One in whose image you were created.

Vision Quest

1. How is your focus? Are you focused inwardly or upwardly toward God? How do you know that you are focused inwardly? What in your life shows you are focused on God?
2. Based on what you read in this chapter, what do fig leaves represent?

3. What are your figs leaves?
4. To whom or what have you been looking to give confirmation of your life vision? Is going back to God confirmation enough for you or do you feel unsettled until the man or woman of God says it is so, or is it your parents, spouse, trusted friend, or other spiritual advisor? Trace the process you take feeling OK about something and determine if God is your source in this area.
5. Why is independent thinking sometimes problematic?

Prayer to Bear His *Image*

Father, I lay down my shame, my fig leaves. I repent for hiding from You. I confess now that I will shift my focus and look to You where my weaknesses, failures, and lack suddenly become insignificant. In the light of Your glory, my nakedness is covered.

I turn my gaze upon You, let me see You for who You are. Move me in position to where I can be trusted with a full vision of Your glory. God, I want to see You.

Amen.

Chapter 5

RESTORING YOUR VISION

HAVE YOU EVER had an eye exam? I'm sure you have, as I have. The interesting thing about one part of the exam is that it seems like they purposely distort your vision to fix your vision. As the strange and blinding combinations of lights and letters, flutter past your eyes, the optometrist asks you, "How is this?" "Is A better, or B?" "A or B?" "B or C?" They may even throw D in for variety. They all look the same to you but feeling under pressure to give an answer before the onslaught of letters and lights begin again, you say, "B!"

Then it starts again, but this time it's numbers. Oh, no. "One or two," the doctor continues. "Two or one." "One or three."

The fear of not getting the combo just right is overwhelming. I mean, you need to be able to see well.

"One!" you announce, partly hoping there is a prize for making a choice.

Getting the right prescription is critical to our livelihood. We use our eyes for almost everything. This same is true for our spiritual vision, yet, we often don't feel the same pressure to get it right as we do at the optometrist's office. I hope that I am making it clear to you how distorted vision can lead to a life of ruin and lack. The inability to see who God truly is and how we were created to reflect that image can affect everything. What we visualize determines what we do. The imagery put before our eyes determines what actions we take on a day-to-day basis. What we believe about God has a direct effect on what we believe about ourselves. What we believe about ourselves affects how we respond to life. God has to adjust our focus and correct our vision so we can see in the spirit with precision and so that our lives will be positioned for the abundant life He died to give us.

In the previous chapters, I had begun to hint to one of the main ways we can be in position for a much-needed vision correction and that is by yielding or submitting ourselves to God. In doing this, God can begin to make the right changes in us so that we rightly reflect His glory. God begins these changes in our character not our personality, as some think. Let me tell you what I mean.

Our personalities have more to do with our behavioral or emotional characteristics—how we respond or interact with people and the things that make up the world around us. For example, one may be an extrovert or introvert; people oriented or task oriented; emotional, introspective, and creative or logical, outgoing, and practical. The gifts of the Spirit function through our unique personality types. For example, a person who has a good sense of humor, when they minister, that humor will be expressed through their delivery style.

Some people have a more artistic or dramatic flair, so when they minister, they use a wide range of vocal inflections, body movements, and facial expressions. People who are detail-oriented and logical may be more monotone and focus on the accuracy of the content they are delivering.

Personality traits are part of the package God put together in us when we were conceived and are as unique as our physical looks and features. You're not sinning because you have brown or blue eyes. Just as being an introvert is not a sin. But, because of sin, of course, each of our personality types have certain weaknesses and this is where we move from personality into character.

When we talk about our character, we are talking about moral and ethical traits we have. It may include things such as integrity, loyalty, kindness, generosity, authenticity, work ethic, and other value systems. Character is what God works on to help adjust our focus.

As we yield our wills over to His, He will begin to change the areas in our characters that our distorted vision has damaged. For some it may be financial stewardship that needs the makeover. For others it could be their health—temperance and self-control or self-worth and the need to see their bodies as temples of the Holy Spirit. Some people have trouble speaking to others in love. When we commit ourselves to the Lord and make time to fellowship with Him, His image is increased and perfected in our eyes and by beholding His true and holy image, those character flaws begin to straighten out and stabilize. Then our values systems are reset to match His. We begin to see others as He sees them.

The make-up of our characters—whether good or bad—determine what we do and how we live. Our actions point to what we truly value. For example, if a person's character flaws include a lack of commitment and faithfulness, if they have a low value of themselves and others, if they are given over to lust, then when they get married, adultery may be their resulting action. Their actions reveal that their image of God's holy institution is distorted. They reveal that they don't hold marriage in the proper and divine light. They don't see it as a mirror of God's and their relationship. It also speaks to how they value their spouse. They don't see them as a precious and honorable child of God. The lack of value they have for marriage exposes their character issues and shines a light on their dysfunctional value system, which points to a distorted view of God and His established order. Do you see the connection?

Their dysfunction and shattered images are also what cause them to miss out on the blessings that come from a committed, loving, and faithful marriage. They and their spouse do not get to walk in dominion as God decreed from the beginning in Genesis 1:28. They do not get to prosper as God intended. They do not walk in their joint purpose together, advancing the kingdom and carrying His glory. The superabundant life that they joined together to live is out of reach because their focus is off.

There are many other dysfunctional circumstances into which a flawed character can lead us. The dysfunction in us is like a magnet. It draws more dysfunction into our lives. We choose dysfunctional relationships because of the dysfunction in us, and we are dysfunctional because the imagery is wrong. We have shattered vision, and it has come from Kleptos. He attempts to pit us against each other. He attempts to influence believers to dishonor each other, to further destroy their God-imagery. Dysfunctional individuals choose dysfunctional mates, and they choose dysfunctional friends. In churches, at workplaces, and in homes, people squabble and get into arguments. They can't walk in unity with each other because they are dysfunctional. The Bible says, "But avoid foolish questions, and genealogies, and contentions, and strivings about the law; for they are unprofitable and vain" (Titus 3:9). And in 2 Timothy 2:24, we learn that a servant of the Lord must not quarrel but be gentle to all" (NKJV).

When our characters are dysfunctional and our vision is blurred, we don't behave as servants of the Lord. We can't operate in love, grace, and compassion. We can't choose relationships that empower and build us, because we're dysfunctional. And if we do find somebody who empowers and builds us, in our dysfunctional state, we are so needy (what I call high maintenance), that we become overwhelming to the other person, so much so, until that other person often stops answering your calls. Dysfunction can cause you to be clingy and approval seeking. Not only troublesome relationships, but also spiritual failure comes from wrong imagery.

We're bombarded by images all day long. From the television to social media to signs on the street, images are created to influence the decisions you make. Images are so strong, in fact, that it's being weighed in US courts the role certain political advertising imagery on Facebook had on the 2016 presidential election results.[1] The images, some say were false, harmful, and accusatory visual ads that led people to vote for one candidate over the other. Whomever you voted for is not the point. This is about how the images we see influence our decisions.

In almost every way, our imagery has been shattered and there must be repair. If you feel rejected, isolated, and have been wrestling against the constant attack of the enemy, he's pressing in one you because he's been able to distort your imagery and he's looking to make the final blow.

If you are going through a divorce, the enemy is going to find ways to make situations and people press your buttons concerning how you feel about yourself. Your spouse may have made you feel as if you weren't good enough or that you weren't enough at all, and their treatment of you produced in you wrong imagery about who you were created to be. Unmarried individuals can often suffer from wrong imagery as the enemy tries to make them feel like they're not beautiful and they are unwanted. Often in both cases, deep insecurity and a sense of unworthiness settles in. These feelings are in conflict with the confidence and victory God has freely given when we behold His image.

Yes, it is true that God created us with thoughts, feelings, emotions, and creativity. Even He has them all. But there has to be a restoration, so that they are all expressed through the lens of God's love for you.

When we come to the Lord, that restorative process is not instantaneously completed in us. Restoration is often a gradual process. It's not completed in one sitting. Second Corinthians 3:18 says, "But we all, with unveiled face, beholding as in a mirror the glory of the Lord, are being transformed into the same image from glory to glory, just as by the Spirit of the Lord" (NKJV). Then in Romans 1:17, it says, "For in it [the gospel] the righteousness of God is revealed from faith to faith" (NKJV). The more the image of God is revealed to us, the more we become like Him. Our initial acceptance of Jesus into our lives is the beginning of that process and it remains ongoing throughout our walk with Him. The more we become like Him, the more we start to see the manifestation of the abundant life.

As a believer you have rights to pursue this transformation and the life that comes as a result. It does not matter what you've done or what mistakes you've made. God's forgiveness runs deep, and His hand is mighty to save. He has a passionate love for you that compels Him to reach to the lowest depths and pull you out from the mess you're in. He will set you upon a rock. He will establish you. He will put a new song in your mouth, and the many who are assigned to experience your gifts and anointing will see it and come to fear and trust the Lord. (See Psalm 40:1–3.)

This is where I want to take you next—the process of getting your vision restored.

IDENTITY: THE KEY TO RESTORED VISION

Merriam-Webster's Dictionary defines *identity* as "the distinguishing character of an individual; the qualities, beliefs, etc., that make a particular person or group different from others."[2] As it pertains to our walk with God, our *identity* is the answer to the question, "Who has God created me to be?" Our *destiny* is the answer to the question, "What has God called me to do?" Your identity is prophetic in that it speaks not only of who you are, but of who you are becoming. It also speaks of the purpose and destiny God has created you for. Living in the light of God's image, we will see both our identity and purpose become clearer.

Our Father wants us to be secure in His love and in who He has created us to be. There are so many believers who are either uncertain or conflicted about their unique personal identity that they find themselves living as poor imitations of someone else rather than living as their authentic selves. There are five clear indications I observed of a person who is uncertain or conflicted about who they are:

1. A lack of personal confidence or self-worth, they are unable to see their own value.
2. Difficulty accepting both their strengths and limitations. They emphasize their faults more than they celebrate their strengths.
3. Being consistently affected by fears, doubts, rejection, or envy. Insecurity plagues them, robbing them of God's peace.
4. Other people's expectations set their direction. They submit to other's expectations even when they sense their direction is wrong.
5. They feel out of place or unfulfilled. They feel like they don't fit in anywhere and that others don't accept them.

Because we can suffer from various types of trauma at some point in our lives and the enemy has made attempts to destroy each one of our images, we all need strengthening, healing, and restoration in the area of our identity. Let's see how to discover who you are in God.

Pointers to Your God-Given Identity

As you begin to make room for God to restore your vision and transform you more into His image, I encourage you to take some time to journal or pray about the points in this section you particularly need strength in.

Your family identity

> Yet to all who did receive him, to those who believed in his name, he gave the right to become children of God.
>
> —JOHN 1:12

Before you can fully comprehend your personal identity, you need to grasp who you are in God's household.

> Now, therefore, you are no longer strangers and foreigners, but fellow citizens with the saints and members of the household of God.
>
> —EPHESIANS 2:19, NKJV

You are the dwelling place of the Spirit of God.

> You also are being built together for a dwelling place of God in the Spirit.
>
> —v. 22

You are royalty.

> But you are a chosen generation, a royal priesthood, a holy nation, His own special people, that you may proclaim the praises of Him who called

> you out of darkness into His marvelous light; who once were not a people but are now the people of God, who had not obtained mercy but now have obtained mercy.
>
> —1 PETER 2:9–10, NKJV

You are beloved and chosen.

> You did not choose Me, but I chose you and appointed you that you should go and bear fruit, and that your fruit should remain, that whatever you ask the Father in My name He may give you.
>
> —JOHN 15:16, NKJV

You are the Father's son or daughter. You carry the family DNA and attributes of God.

> And will be a Father unto you, and ye shall be my sons and daughters, saith the Lord Almighty.
>
> —2 CORINTHIANS 6:18

You are righteous in Christ.

> For he hath made him to be sin for us, who knew no sin; that we might be made the righteousness of God in him.
>
> —2 CORINTHIANS 5:21

It's often when we don't know who we are that we also feel like we don't belong anywhere. As a believer, you belong to the family of God. You have a good and spiritual heritage.

> The lines are fallen unto me in pleasant places; yea, I have a goodly heritage.
>
> —PSALM 16:6

You are one of many members of the body of Christ.

> For as the body is one and has many members, but all the members of that one body, being many, are one body, so also is Christ. For by one Spirit we were all baptized into one body—whether Jews or Greeks, whether slaves or free—and have all been made to drink into one Spirit. For in fact the body is not one member but many.
>
> —1 CORINTHIANS 12:12–14

You are not out there alone. You are not isolated. You belong to the body of Christ. He claims you. He loves you. He is not ashamed of you. He welcomes you. There's so much more that God's Word says about who are. Get before His face and let Him reveal it to you. As we have been discussing, it is vital for you to have a revelation of your identity in Christ. Everything you do depends on it. You cannot be successful in life if you don't know who you are.

Beginning with who God, your Creator, says you are, you will begin to see yourself the way He sees you.

Redeeming Your Vision to Truly See Who You Are

We've discussed this in various forms, but Jesus' whole purpose in coming to Earth was to redeem you from the works of the enemy. Satan has been on a rampage for millennia trying to destroy everything God loves. Jesus came to redeem us from the effects of the destruction of the enemy. As you are studying the Word and praying for a fresh revelation of your identity in God, you will be led at various levels of your transformation process to make these three actions to take advantage of Christ's redemption plan.

These actions are not static—where they happen in precise order or that they even happen all at once. They are fluid and Spirit led. As we come into greater understanding of God's divine image in us, the purity that is developed in our hearts will lead us to walk through these steps as we are led by the Spirit from glory to glory and faith to faith.

1. Repent

> But if we freely admit our sins *when his light uncovers them,* he will be faithful to forgive us every time. God is just to forgive us our sins *because of*

> *Christ,* and he will continue to cleanse us from all unrighteousness.
>
> —1 JOHN 1:9–10, TPT, EMPHASIS ADDED

More than a sorrowful feeling, repentance means to have a change of mind resulting in a change of attitude and behavior. Repentance means we come into agreement with what God has said about the issue. Repentance means making an about-face to go in the opposite direction you were once going. If you were running to alcohol, food, or unhealthy relationships to fill any emptiness, when you repent, you turn around and move toward God. If you were once keeping busy with work to avoid the difficulties in your marriage, when you repent, you close up on time and head home to spend time with your spouse.

Repentance is led by our sorrowful prayers to God, confessing openly to Him and asking for His forgiveness. But it is followed by our Spirit-led actions that help reverse the direction our lives were going.

We have been empowered by Holy Spirit to overcome weaknesses and wrong thoughts, attitudes, and behaviors, which are inconsistent with our kingdom identity. God does not require penitence. Jesus took our sins upon Himself when He went to Calvary. Our sin debt has been paid. God requires repentance.

2. Submit to God

> Submit to God. Resist the devil and he will flee from you. Draw near to God and He will draw near to you. Cleanse your hands, you sinners; and purify your hearts, you double-minded.
>
> —James 4:7–8, NKJV

Submission has to do with our acceptance of our appropriate place in God's order of things. Submit means to yield or surrender to the authority of another. Submit means to make a decision based on trust, to get into the right place.

Submission is also about having enough faith in God, taking Him at His word, and trusting Him to bring His word to pass. When we submit to God, we surrender to the authority of His Word. This causes us, our lives, and our circumstances to line up with what He wills, which is the same as what He says. Therefore, our right place in terms of getting our vision corrected is to live in obedience to God, doing His will.

3. Resist the devil

> Resist the devil and he will flee from you.
>
> —v. 7

Satan has authority to tempt us because of the authority Adam and Eve surrendered in the garden. We have authority to withstand his temptations because of what the Second Adam—Jesus—did to reclaim what they lost.

When we consider ourselves dead to sin and choose not to obey its lusts, we can just say no. (See Romans 6:10–12.) We can walk away from present temptations and any temptations that we are vulnerable to. Through the Holy Spirit, we have the power to resist sin. Sin does not have dominion over us.

If we don't resist the power of sin, we cannot resist Satan. One definition of sin is to miss the mark.[3] When we miss the mark set by God, our sin gives Satan the power to operate in our lives. Has God not said, "Be holy, for I am holy" (1 Pet. 1:6)? Don't let compromises like, "I don't think anything is wrong with this," keep you bound in sin and separated from God. Let it be settled that God's Word sets the standard for our lives.

> Sin is no longer your master, for you no longer live under the requirements of the law. Instead, you live under the freedom of God's grace.
>
> —ROMANS 6:14, NLT

POWER OF PRAYER—REBUILDING THE CONNECTION

Prayer is a part of God's plan for building relationships with us, His children. Prayer is a vital connection between us and God, a time where we not only make our needs known, but we also learn to hear God's voice and commune with Him. Prayer is our opportunity to recreate the fellowship moments Adam and Eve had with God in the cool of the day.

As citizens of God's kingdom, we have been commissioned to produce fruit (John 15:16) and to do His good works (Eph. 2:10). Being fruitful in every good work is reflective of our being in line with God's first command to man in Genesis 1:28:

> Be fruitful and multiply; fill the earth and subdue it; have dominion over the fish of the sea, over the birds of the air, and over every living thing that moves on the earth.
>
> —NKJV

Our fruitfulness and multiplication make us like our Father. We are creators like Him. We are producers like He is. Our mandate is to walk in dominion and subdue the earth. When we walk in the mandate, we are truly reflecting His image. This is the only purpose for our being left on Earth following our salvation and it should drastically change our view of the importance of prayer, communing with God. Here's why.

1. Prayer is the source of life and power.

We cannot produce eternal fruit and fulfill all God's work in our own strength. It is humanly impossible. Good works alone do not necessarily carry eternal value. We need prayer as the lifeline of fellowship with God in order to know His will and receive His strength so that we might produce real fruit in our life (John 15:4–5).

2. Prayer must be cultivated.

Prayer is a discipline that must be cultivated in the life of every believer. Many of us struggle with understanding what to pray for, and as a result, avoid prayer all together. Just as the disciples asked Jesus to teach them to pray, the Holy Spirit will teach you to pray as well. Romans 8:26–27 says,

> In the same way, the Spirit helps us in our weakness. We do not know what we ought to pray for, but the Spirit himself intercedes for us through wordless groans. And he who searches our hearts knows the mind of the Spirit, because the Spirit intercedes for God's people in accordance with the will of God.
>
> —NIV

Here are some tips to help you develop a consistent prayer life:

- Be consistent. Find time each day for prayer. It might be helpful to put prayer in your schedule each day until you find that you are consistently praying daily.
- Consider scheduling prayer in the morning before you begin your day. In so doing, you

are being built up before you are confronted with the issues of the day.

- Include worship music in your times of prayer. Worship music can help to create an atmosphere that will facilitate your times of prayer. You will find it easier to pray when the atmosphere is filled with sounds and songs of heaven. I encourage you to listen to worship music throughout the day to help you remain in the presence of God. This is a way to dwell in the presence of God. Prayer and praise and worship keep you in an atmosphere that mirrors heaven, helping you to overcome distractions and frustrations that arise during your day.
- Pray the Scriptures. Create a list of scriptures that reveal God's heart for you. The Song of Solomon is a great book of the Bible to read since it is about God's love. There are numerous scriptures that declare God's love for us and His power to heal and deliver us. Matthew 6:9–13 contains what is commonly called the Lord's prayer. This prayer is considered a model for prayer and can help you to develop a discipline of prayer.

GOD'S SEERS: SEEK PROPHETIC COUNSEL TO CORRECT YOUR VISION

> Surely the Lord GOD does nothing unless He reveals His secret to His servants the prophets.
>
> —AMOS 3:7

> Your plans will fall apart right in front of you if you fail to get good advice. But if you first seek out multiple counselors, you'll watch your plans succeed.
>
> —PROVERBS 15:21–23, TPT

During the reign of the Old Testament kings of Israel, God assigned His prophets to prophesy to His people. Prophecy is about hearing God's words and delivering them to His chosen subjects. Up until this very day, God continues to use chosen men and women of God to bring His word from heaven to Earth. In ancient Israel, Samuel was the prophet who prophesied during the rule of King Saul. Nathan was the prophet who prophesied during the rule of King David. Isaiah prophesied during the reign of Uzziah, and Jeremiah prophesied during the reign of Josiah. When kings went to war, they sought the counsel of prophets to know whether or not God was with them.

The gift of prophecy has been restored to the church. Ephesians 4:11–13 establishes prophets as part of the government of God:

> And he gave some, apostles; and some, prophets; and some, evangelists; and some, pastors and teachers; for the perfecting of the saints, for the work of the ministry, for the edifying of the body of Christ: till we all come in the unity of the faith, and of the knowledge of the Son of God, unto a perfect man, unto the measure of the stature of the fulness of Christ.

First Corinthians 12:28 lists prophets as second in rank and kingdom order in the church:

> And God hath set some in the church, first apostles, secondarily prophets, thirdly teachers, after that miracles, then gifts of healings, helps, governments, diversities of tongues.

But prophecy is not just something to read about in the Bible. It is for today, and it is a blessing to be part of a ministry or church fellowship where prophetic ministry is valued and promoted. When prophets are welcomed and allowed to flow in their gift, they have the capacity to reveal the heart and will of God in a situation. When making major decisions it can sometimes be difficult to discern the will of God. Receiving the counsel of a prophet provides insight, wisdom, and counsel. Prophetic counsel does not substitute your seeking the Lord personally so that you will know His will for yourself. There will also be areas you may have not heard that will be awakened during prophetic counsel.

All prophecy should be tested and measured against the word of God.

> Do not quench the Spirit. Do not treat prophecies with contempt but test them all; hold on to what is good, reject every kind of evil.
>
> —1 THESSALONIANS 5:19–21, NIV

With the help and counsel of the Holy Spirit, you will become more aware of the areas in your life that need restoration and healing. God wants to restore your image and the image you have of Him. Seeing dimly through a dark glass will only get you so far. Your aim is to be able to sit and gaze upon the beauty of the Lord, to inquire of Him, and get clear direction for your life. Let's continue to the next phase of the restoration process—your image makeover.

Vision Quest

1. What areas in your character do you think God would want to do a makeover?
2. What are some areas in your belief system that cause you trouble when it comes to knowing who you are in God's household?
3. Where are you among the three steps involved with redeeming your vision to see who you truly are? Do you feel

you are where you should be? Why or why not?

4. After reading about the role prayer plays in our connection with God and His vision for us, how does this explain how you see God and yourself in this season of life?
5. Have you ever experienced prophetic ministry? How did it impact your vision? If you haven't experienced prophetic ministry, are you open to it?

Prayer to Bear His *Image*

Thank You, God, for breaking down the middle wall of separation between You and us. Through Your Son, I know I now have direct access to Your throne of grace. Lord, I pray now that as I draw near to You, I will see how You are drawing near to me as You promised in Your Word.

I know that the connection between us could be stronger. I make a new commitment today to seek You more in prayer so that I may draw on Your power to live according to my true identity.

Lord, I also pray that You would send a prophet—Your chosen man or woman—to come and minister to me. I trust and value the gifts in Your church and desire to know Your heart and will. I know prophetic ministry does not replace hearing from You directly. But in whatever way You desire, speak, Lord, for your servant hears. Amen.

Chapter 6

YOUR IMAGE MAKEOVER

I HAD A MAKEOVER not long ago. A department store had sent me a postcard advertising it, so I went in one day during my lunch break to see what they would do with me. This wasn't my first makeover, so I knew how to prepare by not wearing any makeup to allow for an evaluation of my skin to determine the right cosmetics to make my skin and me look our best. This day, though, I had worn lipstick and had mascara on my eyelashes. They used a mild cleanser to remove it, so they had a clean slate to work from.

Afterward I sat in the chair with the details of my face exposed by the bright lights. The makeup artists, or estheticians, looked at my skin, and discussed with me and each other what may work for me and what wouldn't. Once they had a plan, the makeover began. Step by step, they carried out their plan to make me look like a million-dollar woman.

My makeover process was much like the spiritual image makeover we must go through so that the image of God can be clearly seen through us and we look like the image bearers He's destined us to be. In thinking back to my makeover that day, I see that the five-step process the makeup artists and estheticians took me through that day gives a framework for the spiritual makeover process the Lord will take us through once our vision has been corrected. Let's see what that process looks like.

EXFOLIATION OR SLOUGHING OFF

If you have oily skin or have frequent breakouts of acne, the esthetician applies this solution with little granules in it and they begin what is called sloughing off the dead skin. It's a mild abrasive that peels away the dead skin. This is the first step in a spiritual makeover as well, which I call "killing season."

There must be a killing season where the old habits and old ways of thinking are sloughed off. Colossians 3:5 says,

> So kill (deaden, deprive of power) the evil desire lurking in your members [those animal impulses and all that is earthly in you that is employed in sin]: sexual vice, impurity, sensual appetites, unholy desires, and all greed and covetousness, for that is idolatry (the deifying of self and other created things instead of God).
>
> —AMPC

All of the things that need to die in our lives are a result of wrong images that create wrong desires and decisions and lead us in the wrong direction. So, in the first phase of where we need to go in Him, if we're going to begin to look at the adjusted, correct image, we have to be willing to come into a killing season. In this season and by the leading of His Spirit who convicts us of the sin in our lives, we begin to kill or put to death all of those things that are creating the wrong imagery in us. This takes work.

Colossians 3:11 says:

> [In this new creation all distinctions vanish.] There is no room for and there can be neither Greek nor Jew, circumcised nor uncircumcised, [nor difference between nations whether alien] barbarians or Scythians [who are the most savage of all], nor slave or free man; but Christ is all and in all [everything and everywhere, to all men, without distinction of person].
>
> —AMPC

You may struggle with rejection or fear of man. You have to take the Word of God and apply its truth to those lies and encumbrances and begin to slough off. In the last chapter we talked about your identity and allowing God to show you through His Word and revelation from His Spirit who you are. I also mentioned how God's Word sets the standard for living. The truth in His Word will set right all the ideas that have produced wrong imagery in your life. It will cut them off and put them to death, leaving no trace.

> For the word of God is quick, and powerful, and sharper than any two-edged sword, piercing even to the dividing asunder of soul and spirit, and of the joints and marrow, and is a discerner of the thoughts and intents of the heart.
>
> —HEBREWS 4:12

This first step in your spiritual makeover is abrasive and uncomfortable, but you must be willing to go through it to get the beautiful result that God has in store for you. Waiting for you on the other side is the true and full restoration of the image of Christ in you.

The truth of the Word combats the lies of the enemy

There are certain lies the enemy feeds us. Here's a list of some of them. Maybe they sound familiar to you.

- "You're not God's true son or daughter. You're illegitimate."
- "Nobody loves you."
- "You're not the kind of person people like."
- "You are an inferior believer. How is it that everybody else can live right but you?"
- "Your marriage will never change."
- "Your situation will never change."

After years of trying to stand up under these attacks in your own strength, you eventually say, "I guess this is just who I am. This must be how my life was meant to be."

Now, lest you think that this behavior is who you are, God didn't create any of us to be rejected, angry, bitter, hurt, ignored, forgotten, or miserable. He didn't create us to be hopeless, poor, sick, abused, or emotionally broken. He created us in His majestic and glorious image and likeness, and God is not lacking, insecure, unstable, or afraid. He is not Alpha (the beginning) one day and Omega (the end) the next day. He's Alpha and Omega all the time—beginning and the end all the time. His Word tells us that He's unchanging and incapable of lying.

Because of who God is, you can't look at your behavior and say, "Oh, that's just the way I am." If you are made in the image and likeness of God, your dysfunctional life and all that comes with is not just who you are and it is not how your life was meant to be. Repent of those reinforcing and limiting beliefs and let the Word of God renew your thinking. God can change your life. He can deliver you from the demons that torment you. When the demons are removed, your true personality rises up. Your true hopeful, faith-filled, and lovable self emerges. That's who you really are.

> But ye have not so learned Christ; if so be that ye have heard him, and have been taught by him, as the truth is in Jesus: that ye put off concerning the

> former conversation the old man, which is corrupt according to the deceitful lusts; and be renewed in the spirit of your mind; and that ye put on the new man, which after God is created in righteousness and true holiness.
>
> —EPHESIANS 4:20–24

This verse is confirming that we have something to pull off, and we have something to put on. We have to pull off the old, corrupt man and put on the new man which is created in righteousness and true holiness. We must let the Word of God slough off all of the old lies and the old imagery, and then let it cleanse us and wash us and make us holy (Eph. 5:26).

Let the Word wipe the mirror clean.

Have you ever looked into a mirror that was so dusty, smudged with fingerprints, or covered with makeup that you really couldn't see what you were trying to look at? Your natural response is to wipe it clean so that you can see a crystal-clear image. The Word will do this in your life. As you read, study, and pray, it will wipe clean the reflection you are trying to see, which is the image of God.

We used the example in chapter four of going to get your eyes checked, and how they show you distortions to get you to a place where you can see clearly and without distortion. God needs to bring us to a place where we see ourselves without distortion. We need this correction, because when the prophetic word comes around, we will want to be able to believe it and apply it to our lives. If our vision is still distorted when the word of the Lord comes, sometimes that prophecy can overwhelm us. We will hear the great and mighty things the Lord has for us. I mean, it's great destiny and tremendous purpose. But as we stand and look at our shattered image, we say, "This word can't be for me. God isn't going to take me to the nations. I'm going to be a senior leader someday? I can't see myself doing that."

We devalue the prophetic word, because of wrong imagery. So, we must let the Word of God cleanse us and sanctify us. We must let it renew us in the spirit of our minds. We need to let it give us a fresh mental and spiritual attitude, and the only way this can happen is by changing the imagery. The Word is what recreates the accurate image we should see.

Stay out of the funhouse.

The enemy loves to keep you in the house of mirrors. Have you ever been in one of those? It's usually at carnivals and sometimes called the funhouse. It's a room full of mirrors bent in various ways to render all sorts of weird and distorted images. The fun of it is supposed to be about you becoming so disoriented by the many wacky images of yourself that you have a hard time finding your equilibrium and getting out.

Through spiritual attacks and lies against our image and identity, the enemy loves to keep us disoriented, unable to find a firm foundation in who we are. Thank God that the Word says that the eyes of our understanding can be enlightened (Eph. 1:18) and we can be firmly established in God (2 Cor. 1:21)

Come into a new way of thinking.

Vision and thought life are tied together. The developers who created eBay—a new way, at its dawning, to buy and trade online—had rich thought lives: they saw it, they dreamed it, they imagined it, and then they did it. If you read about Richard and Maurice McDonald, the brothers who founded McDonald's, you'll learn that, originally, there was only one restaurant.[1] When they started their restaurant, they had no understanding of how to take their idea to another level so that they could create a chain of restaurants. They wanted to speed up the slow service and they wanted it to be a nice place where lots of people could be served. They first thought of a way for people to drive up to the restaurant to get their meal, so they hired carhops, waitresses who would skate up to the customer's car to take their order and deliver their food. At first, though it seems silly now, they were trying to do this with real china and real drinking glasses. Needless to say, this did not work very well.

In 1948 they revamped everything—new staff, remodeled restaurant and kitchen, and new operating procedures. They streamlined everything. There was no dining room, only a place for people to order and pick up their food. The inexpensive food and super-fast service times brought the customers in droves. By 1954, they had sold twenty-one franchises and opened nine outlets. Two years later, the brothers sold McDonald's to Ray Kroc, a milkshake-machine salesman turned corporate realty agent. He went on to make the corporation a great success, pushing it into what we see now: chains of McDonald's, where they get you in and get you out in under three minutes.[2]

Do you know why this could happen the way it did? Because these men dreamed it, they could see it, and the imagery was there. Their thought lives were open to it and committed to seeing the vision manifest. Their thought lives created vision, vision created destiny, and destiny created wealth.

What you can't see you won't have, but you will have exactly what you see. The way you see yourself today, tomorrow, and in the future, is what determines who you'll be. If you don't see yourself walking in victory, you won't. If you don't see yourself coming out of your situation, you won't. If you don't see yourself standing in the fullness of the call and purposes of God for your life, you won't. We only become what we see. Our thought life and vision are tied together. We must be renewed in the spirit of our mind by engaging with the Word of God.

Verse 24 says: "And put on the new nature (the regenerate self) created in God's image, [Godlike] in true righteousness and holiness" (AMPC).

We make a choice. He says put on, embrace, take this to be who you are now, this nature that is in you. The choice is ours. Will you say yes?

Commit to the Transformation Process

I've never gotten a five-minute makeover. Don't believe them when they tell you they could do it in five minutes. They can't—not a good one. Transformation takes time. Makeovers take time. Spiritual and emotional makeovers take time. Romans 12:1–2 says:

> I appeal to you therefore, brethren, and beg of you in view of [all] the mercies of God, to make a decisive dedication of your bodies [presenting all your members and faculties] as a living sacrifice, holy (devoted, consecrated) and well pleasing to God, which is your reasonable (rational, intelligent) service and spiritual worship.
>
> Do not be conformed to this world (this age), [fashioned after and adapted to its external, superficial customs], but be transformed (changed) by the [entire] renewal of your mind [by its new ideals and its new attitude], so that you may prove [for yourselves] what is the good and acceptable and perfect

> will of God, even the thing which is good and acceptable and perfect [in His sight for you].
>
> —AMPC

We must undergo a complete change, a metamorphosis. We must be fashioned after the image of God. We must put on the new man. We must put on the life of Christ. We must allow our whole entire selves to be made over. If you want to see transformation in your life—whether it's financial, spiritual, marital, relational, physical, or whatever you seek—you must commit to the process.

When I went in to have this makeover, for some silly reason, I thought it was only going to be ten minutes long. I was there an hour-and-a-half. At any given time, I could've gotten up and said, "You know what? I have to go. I can't stay here." I was supposed to have been back to my day a while before. I had other things to do. But if I wanted that makeover, I had to be willing to commit to the process and see it through to the end. If you want transformation in your life, you have got to be willing to commit to the process, because it will not happen overnight. It takes time.

Transformation is painful.

Another thing you need to be prepared for is the pain. Transformation is painful. Most of us say we want to lose weight, you know why many of us haven't? It's painful and it doesn't happen quickly. If you want to see the weight come off, you have to commit to the long, slow, and painful process.

The process to becoming a true image bearer involves a painful death to our old and broken selves. Everything is remade, and we become new. This spiritual transformation brings to life the statement, "No pain, no gain." In this transformation, it first feels like you are losing everything. What you thought was right is being shown as wrong. This process is first about dying, then living.

Jesus says, "For whoever wants to save their life will lose it, but whoever loses their life for me will find it" (Matt. 16:25, NIV). Then in John 12:24, He says, "Very truly I tell you, unless a kernel of wheat falls to the ground and dies, it remains only a single seed. But if it dies, it produces many seeds" (NIV).

If we commit to the process, we will find the image of God we so desperately need to see. We will be restored to a life of fruitfulness and multiplication. The pain is momentarily in the light of eternity and it is worth every moment. Like Christ, we can set our sights on the joy that is set before us (Heb. 12:2). And there it is again. It is all about what we've set our eyes on. Is the pain of transformation worth the joy and abundance that comes from living for God? Is it worth your being able to live at peace despite the attacks of the enemy? Is it worth your being able to know who you are and feeling loved and valued?

Refresh, Restore, and Renew

As I've studied this topic on how to be restored to our position as image bearers, the Holy Spirit led me to Psalm 23:3:

> He refreshes and restores my life (my self); He leads me in the paths of righteousness [uprightness and right standing with Him–not for my earning it, but] for His name's sake.
>
> —AMPC

The Lord was impressing upon me that this verse is referring to a place of renewal, where we are refreshed, energized, and made whole. When I read this verse, it translates to my spirit as, "He restores my soul. He makes new my soul and my entire being."

God performs the ultimate makeover; He makes us entirely new. He brings us to a place of restoration that empowers us for the future. In this place we are empowered to possess everything God has given us. It's the place where rivers of living water flow out of us. That's the image I see when I think of our restored souls. Makeovers bring us to a place of restoration and empowerment.

In this place our hearts are aligned with the kingdom. In the kingdom, there is an image and a likeness by which we are all identified. As we are restored and aligned with God's kingdom, when people look at us, they see God. Before the transformation, there's so much flesh covering over us that

His image can't be seen. But when we go through the makeover, which begins first with sloughing off the dead layers, the image becomes clearer.

The work of restoring the soul is not a work of flesh. It is not a physical labor. It is a spiritual process that we must commit to. We must commit to developing a life of prayer, consecration, and study of the Word. We need all of these things working together. You must read the Word of God and pray, so that the Holy Spirit—our Teacher—will come and illuminate the words so that they become real to you (John 14:26). Sometimes you must pray and fast to break off some of those strongholds and stubborn demonic forces that seem to be hanging on you and your family for dear life (Matt. 17:21). You must commit to a lifestyle of worship so that God will come and dwell in your praise and worship. His presence is everything to a transformed life. All of these dimensions must work together to restore in you the image of God.

You need a vision makeover, because you're looking at wrong images. You're looking at old stuff and past issues, failures, and weakness. As a result, you are feeling like you can't go through and you can't accomplish what God has called you to do. The problem is that, for too long, you've been looking at it in terms of your own strength, what you can do.

You are not alone; we have all done this at some point in our lives. Because of our weaknesses and vulnerabilities, we've hidden ourselves, just as our first parents did. They put on fig leaves; we put on drama, loud talking, addiction, workaholism, and all sorts of other things. But we have to be willing to be naked and unashamed before our Father and allow His image to shine forth. When we peel off flesh—our sinful nature—the image of God begins to shine through and our nakedness is hidden by His glory. Our failures and weaknesses become hidden in His faithfulness and strength.

What to Do If You Slip

There are many times that we can admit to being afraid to start something because we may fail half-way through. Some people won't start a weight-loss plan or a new program of study because they are afraid something will happen and they won't finish. I want to encourage you not to let this be your reason for not committing to God's image makeover. Here's why:

1. God will never fail you.
2. He is faithful to complete all the work He begins in you (Phil 1:6).
3. If you fall a million times, He will pick you up.

> For a just man falleth seven times, and riseth up again
>
> —Proverbs 24:16

> Though he fall, he shall not be utterly cast down: for the LORD upholdeth him with his hand.
>
> —PSALM 37:24

He also uses His church—His body—as His hands and feet to bring aid to His people. So, if you slip or make a mistake, find a mature believer you have confidence in, someone you know who prays, is strong in the Lord, and full of compassion. Be brave and reach out to them. Do not let the enemy talk you into believing this is only an action weak people take. Reaching out for support is one of the strongest things we can do. God created us for community, to connect with and help each other. You can do this. All of the saints in heaven and on Earth are cheering you on.

1. What are some old habits and old ways of thinking you think need to be sloughed off of your life?
2. What lies can you identify that you know are working in your life? It may be hard to think you are simply believing the lies—no one wants to appear that gullible—but even when we don't verbal affirm our belief, our lives can tell on us. Take this time to be open and honest before God.
3. With the list of lies in mind, write a different biblical truth that combats each one.
4. How do you feel when you hear it said that transformation takes time? Some people like quick fixes. Name some

rewarding experiences that you've had where the results took commitment and hard work sustained over a period of time. How did you feel at the culmination of each event? Was the journey worth it?

5. What does the word **restore** mean to you?

Prayer to Bear His *Image*

Lord, as I commit to take this image-makeover journey with You, I thank You in advance for being with me, never failing and never leaving me alone. Thank You for always being there to pick me up if I fall in the past, present, and future.

Continue to restore me to reflect Your image in the earth.

In Jesus' name, I pray. Amen.

Chapter 7

EMBRACE YOUR NEW IMAGE

CLEANSERS, EXFOLIANTS, AND moisturizers applied, the woman began lightly blotting on my foundation and concealer. "How do you like it?" she asked.

Some estheticians ask this several times throughout the makeover. They want to make sure you like what's being done and that you are buying in to your new look. This way, you won't be so quick to revert to your old ways once you get back home. If you don't embrace your new look, you won't keep it. And then what's the point of that?

Toward the end, she handed me the mirror again, stood back to examine her work. "How do you like it?"

"Umm..." I said, as I looked at myself. I didn't want to say what I was thinking.

I looked at myself again. Then I looked at her. She had applied my makeup like she applied her own. Unfortunately, this has been my experience with some female makeup artists. They make you up like they make themselves up.

Most of the time the goal for a makeover is to come out as a better version of yourself. You may have gone with some ideas based on what you saw someone else wear. Generally, you are not hoping to be a clone. Am I right?

God is all about our embracing who He has uniquely created us to be. Embracing our identity in Him is the key to being able to walk in who He says we are. We must embrace the fact that we are accepted in the Beloved (Eph. 1:6). If He says that you are healed and restored, you have to embrace what God has said and live like it is the truth, because it is the truth. You must be willing to embrace the full image of Christ on the inside of you. You are not a loser, but you are a winner. You should declare it to yourself aloud, "I am made in the image and the likeness of God, and that makes me somebody." No matter how many mistakes you make, keep saying, "I am made in the image and the likeness of Christ." You cannot remain defeated once He's set you free. For He who the Son sets free is free indeed (John 8:36). You must overcome the mentality of thinking, "I've fallen, and I can't get up." He upholds you with His right hand. Keep moving forward.

LET GOD CONFIRM WHO YOU ARE

One day with His disciples, Jesus explored His own identity against who He knows He is, who His disciples thought He was, and who people guessed He was.

> "Who do men say that I, the Son of Man, am?"
>
> So they said, "Some say John the Baptist, some Elijah, and others Jeremiah or one of the prophets."
>
> He said to them, "But who do you say that I am?"

> Simon Peter answered and said, "You are the Christ, the Son of the living God."
>
> Jesus answered and said to him, "Blessed are you, Simon Bar-Jonah, for flesh and blood has not revealed this to you, but My Father who is in heaven.
>
> —Matthew 16:13–17

People will always have an opinion concerning who they think you are. But Jesus shows us that, even in His own experience as a human, God is the one who reveals and confirms who we are. Jesus made a point here: don't depend on people to identify you; let God's Word do that.

Embrace Your Garment

There's another story I remember hearing when I was a child. It's based on an old fable from the 1800s written by Hans Christian Anderson called *The Emperor's New Clothes*.[1] It has also been made into a Disney movie by the same name. Throughout history people have used the phrase, "the emperor has no clothes," to support many valid points about deception. The phrase originates with this story, but for our purposes here I want to offer a different perspective.

The tale is about an emperor who loved to wear new clothes. One day two weavers came to town and told him about some special fabric they used that revealed honest and honorable men. The emperor was intrigued, paid their expensive price, and agreed to have them make him a new suit. They began working immediately making the emperor's new garment.

The strange thing was nobody could see the garment, even after several days of work. But the weavers were continually sewing. Now, I'm sure he paid for that suit. When the big day came for him to wear it, the people were shocked. "You don't have any clothes on," they yelled.

The emperor wouldn't believe it was true. The weavers worked hard on his clothes night and day. He paid them a pretty nickel. When he took his clothes off to put his new garments on, he knew they had dressed him finely. So even as the people gasped, he marched out there with his head held high.

The moral to my version of the story is this: sometimes the changes in you are not readily seen by other people, but you must be willing to embrace your garment. The emperor embraced his invisible clothes, and he walked right out in front of all his subjects. The idea of it seems funny, doesn't it? Can you imagine? But how funny is it when friends from your past look at you and laugh, when you say, "God's going to use me in prophecy," "I'm going to be an author," or "God's called me to start a church."

Sometimes when you tell people who God has called you to be, they laugh. But if you commit to the process of transformation, sooner or later, they're going to stop laughing.

When my husband and I first started our church, people said it wasn't going to grow. They said we'd quit and go home.

After the second year, they said the same thing. They said since I was so visible as a woman pastor, men would not want to be part of our church. But God started sending men to the church.

Every negative thing people said was going to happen didn't. Everything they said wouldn't happen, God started doing it. Then after the seventh year, everybody stopped laughing. Now everybody's serious. We never gave up and even though other people couldn't see who we were or the mantle we were dressed in, we embraced the garment God had fashioned for us.

When you embrace what God has said for you—what He has clothed you in—and you don't allow other people's opinions to distort the image, you will achieve success, because you have embraced the image of God at work in you. You have to know you're royalty. You have to march out there with your head held high and declare, "I am a king, "I am a queen," "I am seated in heavenly places with Christ Jesus. I'm going to wear the garment God has for me." You must reject the image the enemy is trying to create in you. The attacks of the enemy occur each day, and you must commit to rejecting the makeover he is offering you.

DO NOT FALL FOR WHAT YOU SEE WITH YOUR NATURAL EYES

This is a season when God really wants you to experience restoration in every broken place, but you must commit to the process. There must be a killing season. A killing season occurs when you commit to putting to death wrong ways of thinking that create wrong perceptions of who you are. There must be a new way of thinking. Vision and thought life link together.

When you understand that the image of God is at work on the inside of you, no devil in hell can overcome you. Second Corinthians 3:18 says, "And all of us, as with unveiled face, [because we] continued to behold [in the Word of God] as in a mirror the glory of the Lord, are constantly being transfigured into His very own image in ever increasing splendor and from one degree of glory to another; [for this comes] from the Lord [Who is] the Spirit" (AMPC).

God's glory is revealed as you study His Word, as you come into that place of fellowship. Many times, it's hard to get there because you are so locked into the natural realm. You are so locked into what you can see with your natural eyes. And sometimes, if you let the devil play with your mind, he'll have you wondering if God is real. He'll set the whole thing up again like he had it in the garden: "Could it really be that God is even real? Could it really be that there's nothing on the other side of eternity? Could it really be or is death the end of it all? How do you know that heaven is real? You've never seen it."

If your prayer life is at a zero and you've never ascended into heaven to experience any of the activity in heaven, you will believe the devil is telling you the truth. Just as he did with Eve, he will cause you to doubt that God is telling you the truth and lead you on a search for "truth" outside of God. The lies of the enemy will seduce you into believing that your current state is unchangeable. Don't forget that the enemy is the father of lies.

There was a young man I once knew who said that the devil told him he would make him rich if he stopped serving God. The people around me who heard him say it said, "Do you understand what you just said?"

He said, "Yes. The devil told me he's going to make me rich if I stop serving God."

He did it. He returned to his former life, committed a crime for which he was caught and convicted. The riches he received was jail time.

We can become deceived by what we see with our natural eyes. Everything we see with our natural eyes will soon fade. It's only temporal, but the invisible things are the things that are real. We must be willing to pull off flesh and behold His glory. As we behold Him, we are transformed because we are looking into Him as we would a mirror. We are being transformed into the same image we see.

GROW UP IN HIM

As we behold the glory of the Lord, we mature. We grow up in Him in all things. Let us welcome the transformation and allow His glory and His Word to renew the spirit of our mind. Let us take off immaturity and begin to grow up in God. Let your ministry be something where people can begin to grow up in Him in all things. Let your business prosper, where people are served with excellence and integrity. Let your relationships be ones where your friends and family are refreshed, supported, and accepted. Let your career blossom, so your employers know there is a believer in their employ. Not only does their profit margin increase, but there is also peaceful interpersonal interactions as a result of who you are in Christ. This is how maturity in God can show up in practical ways in every area of your life.

But this is only the beginning. So much more than you could ask or image is in store for you because you love God. We need to be exposed to the image of God more and more. We need our flesh to be sloughed off so that the glory of His presence can radiate from us. From faith to faith and glory to glory, we are increasing and becoming more like Him. His image shining through us will give life to all those around us.

BE ONE WHO LOOKS LIKE GOD

Your season for being restored to the glorious image of God is here. You are part of the ones whom God is creating to look like Him in this hour. You are His child. You have been adopted into His family. And just like in our natural families, you have, in the spirit, begun to look like your heavenly Father. Don't be afraid to let His image shine through you.

If you are a husband reading this book, I encourage you to pray that more of the image of God will be reflected in your life with your wife and your children. If you are a wife, I encourage you to pray that your husband and your children can see more of the image of God in you. If you are a parent, I encourage you to pray so that your children can see more of the image of God at work in you. As an employee or businessowner, let it be that the people that you work with see more of the image and the likeness of God at work on the inside of you, because when they do, they will come to Him too. They desire God more than they know.

> Look with wonder at the depth of the Father's marvelous love that he has lavished on us! He has called us and made us his very own beloved children. The reason the world doesn't recognize who we are is that they didn't recognize him. Beloved, we are God's children right now; however, it is not yet apparent what we will become. But we do know that when it is finally made visible, we will be just like him, for we will see him as he truly is. And all

> who focus their hope on him will always be purifying themselves, just as Jesus is pure.
>
> —1 JOHN 3:1–3

You've come to this book for such a time as this. It was not a coincidence that the title, cover, or whatever it was drew you to read it. God wants you to be the very image of His glory in the earth. We need beauty, grace, power, and strength displayed now more than ever. It's all in you ready to burst forth.

Vision Quest

1. What are some of the things you know God has called you to that others find hard to believe? Do you feel their disbelief has held you back? What ways can you see this is true? If it has not held you back, what keeps you moving forward?
2. What are some of the safeguards you are going to put in place to avoid relying on what you see with your natural eyes? Write out a plan so that you have something to come back to when life makes it hard to see God's vision.
3. Write a vision or mission statement for your ministry, business, career, or personal life that demonstrates your maturity in God. What attributes of God's character would you like to be seen in that area, so people know they have been served by an image bearer?
4. What relationships will you commit to prayer so that you

look like God to those significant ones? In what ways can you improve the image you are reflecting?

5. Write a prayer of commitment to continue this journey of reflecting God's image in the earth. There will always be room for you to grow in this area as God reveals more of Himself to you in the days and months to come. Finally, in your prayer, thank God for seeking you out to bring you a 20/20 vision for your life in Him. What a privilege.

Prayer to Bear His *Image*

Father, I bless You and thank You. I thank You for making me in Your image and likeness. Father, I pray for a greater revelation of how your image is transforming me and everything in my life day by day. I pray for understanding. God, I pray that, with an unveiled face, I will behold You face to face. Let me see Your image. Let me see that it is at work on the inside of me. Let me not shrink back from the sometimes painful and long process of transformation. Lord, with Your help, I commit to see myself changed into the image bearer You've created me to be. In Jesus' name, I pray. Amen.

NOTES

Chapter 1—The Power of Imagery

1. Merriam-Webster.com, s.v. "image," https://www.merriam-webster.com/dictionary/image.
2. Merriam-Webster.com, s.v. "imagination," https://www.merriam-webster.com/dictionary/imagination.
3. Gonzalo Sanchez, "Why People Love Grate Visuals, Based on Science," Piktochart.com, https://piktochart.com/blog/why-people-love-great-visuals-science/.
4. Ibid.
5. Andrew Tate, "10 scientific reasons people are wired to respond to your visual marketing," https://www.canva.com/learn/visual-marketing/.
6. Ibid.
7. Ibid.
8. Salk Institute. "Brain's Response to Visual Stimuli Helps Us to Focus on What We Should See, Rather Than All There Is to See," ScienceDaily. www.sciencedaily.com/releases/2005/10/051023121255.htm.

Chapter 2—After His Likeness

1. Merriam-Webster.com, s.v. "image," https://www.merriam-webster.com/dictionary/image.
2. BlueLetterBible.org, s.v. "*tselem*," https://www.blueletterbible.org/lang/lexicon/lexicon.cfm?Strongs=H6754&t=KJV.

3. Merriam-Webster.com, s.v. "icon," https://www.merriam-webster.com/dictionary/icon.
4. BlueLetterBible.org, s.v. "*eikon*," https://www.blueletterbible.org/lang/lexicon/lexicon.cfm?Strongs=G1504&t=KJV.
5. BlueLetterBible.org, s.v. "*zoe*," https://www.blueletterbible.org/lang/lexicon/lexicon.cfm?Strongs=G2222&t=KJV.
6. Ibid.
7. BlueLetterBible.org, s.v. "*perissos*," https://www.blueletterbible.org/lang/lexicon/lexicon.cfm?Strongs=G4053&t=KJV.
8. BlueLetterBible.org, s.v. "*kleptes*," https://www.blueletterbible.org/lang/lexicon/lexicon.cfm?Strongs=G2812&t=KJV.

CHAPTER 3—IMAGE ROBBER

1. BlueLetterBible.org, s.v. "*kleptes*," https://www.blueletterbible.org/lang/lexicon/lexicon.cfm?Strongs=G2812&t=KJV; s.v. "klepto," https://www.blueletterbible.org/lang/lexicon/lexicon.cfm?Strongs=G2813&t=KJV.
2. Ibid.
3. Merriam-Websters.com, s.v. kleptomaniac, https://www.merriam-webster.com/dictionary/kleptomania.
4. BlueLetterBible.com, s.v. "*thyo*," https://www.blueletterbible.org/lang/lexicon/lexicon.cfm?Strongs=G2380&t=KJV
5. Ibid.
6. Ibid.

Chapter 4—Out of Focus

1. *The Wizard of Oz,* directed by Victor Fleming (1936; Beverly Hills, CA: Metro-Goldwyn-Mayer).
2. *Shallow Hal,* directed by Bobby Farrelly and Peter Farrelly (2001; Los Angeles, CA: Twentieth Century Fox).

Chapter 5—Restoring Your Vision

1. Alana Abramson, "Facebook Says Russian Accounts Bought $100,000 in Ads During the 2016 Election," http://time.com/4930532/facebook-russian-accounts-2016-election/.
2. Merriam-Webster.com, s.v. "identity," https://www.merriam-webster.com/dictionary/identity.
3. BibleHub.com, s.v. "266. *hamartia,*" https://biblehub.com/greek/266.htm.

Chapter 6—Your Image Makeover

1. Kenneth N. Gilpin, "Richard McDonald, 89, Fast-Food Revolutionary," NYTimes.com, July 16, 1998, https://www.nytimes.com/1998/07/16/business/richard-mcdonald-89-fast-food-revolutionary.html.
2. Ibid.

Chapter 7—Embrace Your New Image

1. H. C. Andersen Centre, "The Emperor's New Clothes," http://www.andersen.sdu.dk/vaerk/hersholt/TheEmperorsNewClothes_e.html.

CPSIA information can be obtained
at www.ICGtesting.com
Printed in the USA
LVHW081405301221
706603LV00003BA/15